Praise for *The Leadership Compass*

Michelle's genuine and relatable approach to sharing her experiences in business and sports makes *The Leadership Compass* a must-read for women who are ready to take charge of their careers. This book is a game-changer! As a black immigrant woman, navigating the corporate world often left me feeling adrift, encountering setbacks that seemed insurmountable. However, Michelle's astute insights and practical advice have helped turn my head a few degrees, allowing me to see possibilities that were in my blind spot before.
Amal Yusuf | GM Airport Operations, Delta Air Lines

Michelle has been successfully challenging and inspiring women to step into and realise their leadership potential for many years. I've seen her insights resonate with women at every stage of their career journey and have significant personal and organisational impact. I am grateful to have experienced and supported her leadership programs first-hand and to now have this knowledge in a book to share more widely!
Carol-Ann Gough | CIO, Great Southern Bank

Michelle Redfern is a refreshing voice in the equity space. There is no beating around the bush or mincing words – Michelle tells it like it is, and I was delighted in reading this book that she writes as she speaks. Michelle has a knack of being able to engage with people from shop floor to executive, and her book will be universally appealing for this very reason.
Bronwyn Woods | Head of Organisational Development, Bega Group

Michelle's leadership experience is vast and her wisdom is deep. We're blessed that she's put her knowledge down in this practical and extremely well-researched guide. Every page brings useful information that is immediately actionable, with excellent self-inquiry work that is illuminating for understanding your own leadership skills. I love that Michelle addresses all stages of our leadership journey, from early in our career to C-level. And most of all, her customary pull-no-punches way of speaking truth about the systemic gender inequality that limits women's potential is, as always, glorious. *The Leadership Compass* is a critical handbook for women seeking to advance their own leadership and organisations who need more women leaders.
Jo Stanley | CEO, Broad Radio; media expert and author

The Leadership Compass is a breath of fresh air in the conversation about women in leadership. In a world where busyness often hinders progress, Michelle Redfern guides women to focus their time and attention on what truly matters for advancing into and thriving in senior positions. Concise yet packed with substance, this book empowers women and challenges the narrative that they need 'fixing', highlighting instead the necessity of systemic changes for real progress in gender equity.

Melanie Ho | Author, *Beyond Leaning In*

The importance of developing business intelligence and understanding the financial drivers of a business cannot be underestimated and must be an area of focus for women aspiring to leadership. *The Leadership Compass* shines a light precisely on where to focus and provides timely and practical resources to help women apply learnings. Bravo Michelle Redfern!

Nickie Scriven | CEO, Chief Meta Chicks

The Leadership Compass provides a practical roadmap for women seeking to meet their career ambitions. Michelle's engaging style, personal anecdotes and tips will make you smile but also realise the importance of pragmatically focusing on business, financial and strategic acumen in order to succeed in your career.

Corinne Proske | CEO, Trust for Nature

Michelle Redfern acutely understands the tenets of good leadership and why women's participation at the top is key to Australia's overall social and economic success. This book provides a brilliant step-by-step guide on climbing the ladder and fulfilling your purpose.

Tarla Lambert | Editor in Chief, *Women's Agenda*

The Leadership Compass fills the gap that a lot of women miss when undergoing traditional leadership courses. Michelle stresses the importance of needing to change the system, not the women. She walks through her process in a witty and honest way, which really helps you connect with the author and the material. I feel that this book should be recommended reading for both women and men at FanDuel.

Juliette Gorson | Data Science Senior Manager, FanDuel

THE LEADERSHIP COMPASS

The ultimate guide for *Women leaders* to reach their full potential

THE LEADERSHIP COMPASS

Michelle Redfern

MAJOR
STREET

This book is dedicated to the women who have been a compass throughout my life and taught me how women's leadership shows up: Nana, Mum, my sisters, my daughter, my nieces and my aunties. But, most of all, this book is a tribute to the woman who has helped me unlock the best version of myself: my beloved wife Rhonda.

MAJOR STREET

First published in 2024 by Major Street Publishing Pty Ltd
info@majorstreet.com.au | +61 421 707 983 | majorstreet.com.au

© Michelle Redfern 2024
The moral rights of the author have been asserted.

A catalogue record for this book is available
from the National Library of Australia

Printed book ISBN: 978-1-922611-99-4
Ebook ISBN: 978-1-923186-00-2

Cover design by Tess McCabe
Internal design by Production Works

10 9 8 7 6 5 4 3 2 1

Contents

Foreword by
Susan L Colantuono

It was 2016 and I was CEO of Leading Women, a renowned global firm delivering leadership development programs for women and gender dynamics training for managers. As part of my strategy to further extend its reach, I was negotiating with a consulting firm in Australia for whom my IP was complementary.

Now, if you're one of the more than 4.4 million viewers of my TED Talk, 'The Career Advice You Probably Didn't Get', you know that my IP is truly revolutionary. I had discovered what I called 'The Missing 33%™ of the career success equation for women' and the ways that it served as a barrier to women's advancement – in terms of both what women were told we had to do to soar in our careers *and* what most managers delivered to women on the rare occasions they chose to nurture or support our ambitions.

In essence, The Missing 33%™ was (and based on my 2023 updated research, still is) women's perceived – and in some cases actual – lack of business, financial and strategic acumen.

Given the centrality to my leadership programs of The Missing 33%™ and related content to build business, financial and strategic acumen, I had very specific criteria for who would be sufficiently qualified to deliver them. Therefore, when the Australian firm said they would identify a woman who would deliver my programs, I insisted on the criteria being met. This was to prevent career-advice-as-usual syndrome from drowning out my messages about the importance of The Missing 33%™ and avoiding the programs devolving into the typical 'management training with a dose of work-life balance' that permeates the women's leadership development industry.

I rejected a number of candidates for lacking actual executive leadership experience, and then they served up the resume of someone named Michelle Redfern.

Wow, I thought, she's definitely been the operational and strategic executive that I'm looking for. If she's personable, good in front of people and believes in my message, she could be the perfect woman to deliver my programs in Australia and New Zealand.

We actually met when Michelle travelled to the US to observe one of my programs. They were right. She was perfect!

She was brilliant, dynamic, personable, open-minded and a staunch feminist with corporate career and leadership success experiences that, when put into my model, provided insights about her career success that made perfect sense.

When she arrived in New Jersey to observe the delivery of one of my programs for women in middle management, our mutual admiration was cemented and our working relationship began in earnest. She delivered programs for Leading Women to great accolades, developed her own successful consulting practices and, when I later launched Lead to Soar, the online network for ambitious women, Michelle took over as owner. In the years since we met, I was awed as Michelle added her own personal experiences, insights and models to my IP in order to make huge differences in the careers of women around the world and the organisational cultures within which they work.

Fast-forward to 2023. Michelle tells me she is writing a book. I'm thrilled beyond belief. Her messages about the importance of business intelligence (BQ), emotional intelligence (EQ) and social intelligence (SQ) are crucial to you and others like you who aren't able to attend a program with her. Because she adds so much to conventional wisdom about all three areas, the content deserves much wider exposure than Michelle could possibly deliver through her extensive LinkedIn following, her Lead to Soar network and podcast, and her Advancing Women consulting business.

Reading chapters 2 and 3, for example, reminded me of how an oyster adds layers of shining beauty to a central grain of sand. If my work on the importance of business, financial and strategic acumen is that central grain of sand, Michelle's further insights are creating a glorious pearl to lay in your hands and those of other women around the globe!

Then, the pièce de résistance: in chapter 10, Michelle steps forward to tackle the fundamental truth that cracking the secret to women's advancement requires managers and organisational cultures to change. She goes further to explain why and how.

Throughout it all, Michelle's shares personal experiences and 'Go deeper' guidance to add the real-world grounding and actionable advice that transforms *The Leadership Compass* from simply another book into an ambitious woman's career companion. It's truly the ultimate guide for women leaders who seek to reach their full potential and for organisations that seek to create conditions to make that possible.

You might think that my comments are biased because of our working relationship – and, of course, they are. *But*, every day inside the Lead to Soar network and throughout my LinkedIn feed I see women from all over the world, from individual contributors to CEOs, from all different professions and industries, express gratitude for Michelle's coaching and wise insights. The feedback she receives from participants in her leadership programs is extraordinary, and many of the women I know who've participated have gone on to ever more rewarding careers.

Still wondering if *The Leadership Compass* is worth the read? Dive in. Your career aspirations will thank you!

Susan L Colantuono
Founder of Be Business Savvy and author of *No Ceiling, No Walls* and *Make the Most of Mentoring*

Preface

I Am a Leader

For much of my career, I struggled to give myself a label because I felt I wasn't anything. I'm not a doctor, engineer, firefighter, hairdresser, lawyer, accountant or any other type of professional with a certification and a prescribed set of technical proficiencies. However, while I did eventually gain a degree, I realised I already had a vocation with technical proficiencies.

I am a leader.

When I became conscious of the importance of leadership and the skills needed to be the best leader I could be, I became more deliberate about exposing myself to, and inserting myself into, situations and environments where I could learn how to be a great leader. That included watching, talking to and learning from leaders near and far away. It involved reading many books, particularly biographies of leaders, so I could discover the secret sauce of leadership. It meant attending conferences and events where keynote speakers would expound on the virtues of great leadership and how to 'do' leadership well. It led me to put my hand up for any training courses and professional development opportunities that came my way.

I also learned on the job and from the leaders I reported to, and sought out opportunities to stretch and grow through the new leadership roles I applied for and was appointed to.

One thing characterised my leadership journey: I learned my leadership craft largely from men. Why? Because I didn't have a woman boss (at the executive level) until I was a senior manager in my late 30s. Given I'd been in the paid workforce from the age of 15, that's a lot of years learning from a lot of blokes.

When I look at the representation of women in CEO and executive roles worldwide in 2023, there are certainly more women than when I started navigating my career, but still not enough. Men still dominate leadership.

The political sphere, arguably the most powerful and influential leadership sphere in the world, is dominated by men. Just 13 out of the 193 member states in the United Nations have women as heads of state.

Similarly, when I consider the biographies of successful leaders across all sectors, men still dominate the titles. It is the same for business books. And don't get me started on the speaking circuit and the media – when it comes to talking about leadership and business, men dominate there, too.

The paucity of women in these arenas means that women today are still learning the craft of leadership from one relatively homogenous group. And that is just not good enough.

The leadership compass

When people ask me what I do, I tell them that I do three things:

1. I fix workplace systems that prevent women and organisations from reaching their full potential.
2. I help women navigate the systems in their workplace to reach their full potential. I am like a human compass to guide women towards success.

3. I advocate for the rights of women and girls, particularly in the sporting sector.

Each of these pillars ensures I live my purpose: to close the global leadership gender gap in my lifetime.

This book is a compass to help women navigate more rapidly towards leadership at every level with guidance from a woman who has been there and done that. It is also a tool to enable those already in leadership positions with great authority and influence to take action to close the leadership gender gap in their organisation.

But most importantly, this book is a no-holds-barred look at leadership through the lens of my career as a woman who is, and always has been, a leader.

Introduction

Business, Emotional and Social Intelligence

Leaders who aim for a successful career should have a good grasp of business intelligence (BQ), emotional intelligence (EQ) and social intelligence (SQ). This introduction provides insights into my approach to leadership. Additionally, it outlines the system I use to support women who aspire to advance their leadership careers and organisations that seek to harness the benefits of having more women in their leadership ranks.

Before I expand on this system, I want to credit two people who have inspired me with their approaches to leadership. One of these people, Susan Colantuono, I know well and is a friend, colleague and mentor. The other, Dr Daniel Goleman, I do not know personally, but I have avidly consumed his articles, books, podcasts and other content to become the best version of myself in life and leadership. I am a more evolved human and leader due to my deep commitment to leadership excellence.

I had been running my business as a side hustle for about ten months when an opportunity was presented to me: a leadership training organisation I was a repeat client of approached me to join them. This consultancy had discovered I that was leaving my executive career and starting a business to advance women in the workplace. They wanted to collaborate with me as they set up a practice within their very male-dominated organisation to target women's leadership development in the corporate sector.

The consultancy had identified Susan Colantuono, who had been researching and developing leadership programs specifically aimed at women for over 15 years. She had a TED Talk, 'The Career Advice You Probably Didn't Get', and several books published. The consultancy would license some of the content Susan Colantuono had developed for use in Australia and New Zealand.

Part of my onboarding to this organisation was to fly to the USA to meet Susan and be trained in her content and delivery. So, I went to New Jersey, not knowing that this would be one of the most important events of my career.

On my long flight to New York I watched the TED Talk and read two of Susan's books: *No Ceiling, No Walls: What women haven't been told about leadership from career-start to the corporate boardroom* and *Make the Most of Mentoring: Capitalize on mentoring and take your career to the next level*.

In New Jersey I observed one of Susan's leadership programs being delivered over two days to 25 middle management women at one of the largest telcos in the USA. Light bulb after flashing light bulb was going off in my head as I sat at the back of that training room. I was furiously scribbling notes and contemplating the truth bombs that kept coming. And I got mad that the information I was hearing hadn't been shared with me before.

This was the information that was setting off all these light bulbs and making me mad: that business, strategic and financial acumen are essential skills for women who want to advance in their careers (light bulb), and 97% of the career advice, coaching, mentoring, leadership training and literature aimed at women fails to overtly address the importance of building and demonstrating these skills (mad).

This is BQ. Women must be *known as* leaders with abundant BQ to ensure career success and advancement to the highest level. I emphasise 'known as' because BQ is next to useless for career advancement unless those making decisions about your advancement know that you possess and utilise the competencies required for advancement to the next level.

After the session, I approached Susan and almost wailed, 'I needed you, and this, 25 years ago!' She responded wisely, 'You are here now, and that's what matters'.

It mattered because while I'd had a very successful career, I realised how lucky I had been to have managers who had deliberately ensured that I developed and demonstrated very strong BQ skills. These BQ skills and my continuously developing EQ skills had positioned me as a businesswoman who 'got it' and could remediate, optimise or transform whatever business she was given carriage over. Now, it was my turn to gain more skills to share Susan's work and my career experiences with other women to accelerate their career progression.

I now knew that I was successful because I was known as a businesswoman who tapped into all three components of Susan's leadership definition: 'Leadership is using the greatness in you to achieve and sustain extraordinary outcomes by engaging the greatness in others'.

Achieving and sustaining extraordinary outcomes is BQ. It means managing yourself and others to achieve strategic and financial outcomes for your organisation. It means you understand what keeps the CEO and CFO awake at night, and you act as part of your leadership commitment to continuously ensure the organisation's success. It also means you are committed to learning and developing essential leadership behaviours that enable you to create and sustain high-performance teams and organisations.

I was now part of a movement to ensure that more women in more workplaces knew the importance of BQ in leadership.

The importance of business intelligence (BQ) in leadership

Susan Colantuono has educated and inspired me to ensure that women are made aware of the importance of a multifaceted approach to leadership and pay attention to building and demonstrating critical business skills. Even now, as Susan wrote in *No Ceiling, No Walls*, 'Women haven't been told about the importance of business skills to their success'. I have facilitated hundreds of workshops with women since 2017, and I am still confronted by the fact that women are simply not advised, coached, mentored and trained to understand the importance of having and demonstrating BQ.

Susan discusses the importance of having and demonstrating three core competencies:

1. **Business acumen** is the ability to understand a business's overall health and performance. It means you know your business – how it generates cash, achieves profitable growth, delights its customers, pleases shareholders and develops engaged and productive team members.

2. **Strategic acumen** is the ability to develop and execute long-term plans for the business. This means you can see the big picture and the long-term implications of your decisions.

3. **Financial acumen** is the ability to understand the financial performance of a business and the story that the numbers tell. You know how to assess the financial health of your organisation by reading and analysing its financial and performance metrics, and then to take action based on your understanding.

Women still face barriers to advancement in business, and I want to help. Susan's ongoing research, as well as mine, reliably informs us that developing BQ will make a big difference in career growth for women.

When you read Chapter 2: Leadership that Gets Results and Chapter 3: Metrics that Matter, you will gain an insight into just how profoundly Susan's decades of work have influenced me and the work that I do – both with organisations, to help them close their leadership gender gaps, and directly with ambitious women who want to soar!

I attribute much of the success I have enjoyed in my entrepreneurial journey to Susan. Her work inspires this book, pays homage to her trailblazing research and continues to build the body of work by women for women to advance their careers.

Thank you, Susan, for your wisdom, and generosity to me as I follow your blazing trail and, of course, for the wonderful friend you are.

The importance of emotional intelligence (EQ) in leadership

Dr Peter Salovey and Dr John D Mayer developed the psychological theory of emotional intelligence, writing in 1997, 'Emotional intelligence is the ability to perceive emotions, to access and generate emotions so as to assist thought, to understand emotions and emotional knowledge, and to reflectively regulate emotions so as to promote emotional and intellectual growth'.

However, Dr Daniel Goleman arguably popularised EQ and brought it into mainstream business and leadership theory. Goleman put 'emotional intelligence' on the bestseller list and has authored several books on the subject, including *Emotional Intelligence: Why it can matter more than IQ*, *Working With Emotional Intelligence* and *Social Intelligence: The revolutionary new science of human relationships*. Goleman's work has also inspired both my own development and now the development of other women leaders, specifically around the importance of emotional intelligence.

I don't recall when I first started reading Goleman's content, but I recall that when studying for one of the leadership modules for my Executive MBA, one of my assigned readings was 'Leadership That Gets Results', a *Harvard Business Review* article by Goleman. Lightning bolt! Goleman discussed effectiveness as a leader and the importance of understanding and adopting a range of leadership styles to be effective at any given moment, depending on the circumstances. The six leadership styles he outlines allowed me to audit my approach to leadership.

This was an important breakthrough for me as I had seen myself as a leadership chameleon: I adapted my style and approach to suit the circumstances at hand, but as a result I grappled at times with feelings of inauthenticity or, worse, duplicity. Thanks to this newfound knowledge, I had a reference point for behaviours that meant I was having the right conversation with the right person at the right time about the right thing! I also realised that while I considered myself a leader with well-developed EQ skills, I viewed them through a narrow, incomplete prism.

So, what is the 'recipe' for demonstrating high EQ in leadership? According to Goleman, 'Emotional intelligence includes self-mastery (self-awareness and self-regulation), plus social intelligence (empathy and social skill). Both are essential: you have to lead yourself before you can lead others'.

In chapters 4, 5 and 6, you will discover how, through well-developed EQ skills, you can lead yourself first, then lead others and organisations.

As our world grows more complex and connected, it's clear that EQ will play an increasingly important role in effective leadership. When I am facilitating my workshops, I make a joke (that is actually serious) about the expectations of leaders today. I say that when I started my leadership journey 947 years ago (ha-ha), my duties were largely about supervising and management. Fast-forward to the 21st century and we now expect leaders not only to understand and manage their own emotions but also to navigate the emotions of those around them to build successful teams and organisations. This takes significant skill and a commitment to ongoing development.

It really annoys me that EQ skills, which are often referred to as 'soft skills', are perceived as not being as valuable as technical or practical skills. What a load of old cobblers! Emotional intelligence is as critical to leadership and business as 'hard' skills or technical competencies.

The importance of social intelligence (SQ) in leadership

In addition to Colantuono and Goleman, there is a third person who inspires me with their approach to leadership: me. Allow me to toot my own horn when it comes to demonstrating SQ. The final chapters in the book will highlight the skills and competencies associated with SQ, which I am proud to say I am largely self-taught in, driven by my innate curiosity about how to stand out and make an impact no matter what I am doing.

I am no shrinking violet and am a very confident woman, but that has not always been the case, and there have been several occasions during my life when I've had to draw on some inner strength to meet challenges head-on. I'll expand on some of those in the following chapters. However, one story needs telling now; it demonstrates how having the right mindset can help you attain the necessary skills for success.

In early 2005, I resigned from Telstra after 15 years of service. Many of my colleagues thought I was mad because, first, I was resigning and not taking a redundancy package, and second, I had a very positive career trajectory in front of me. So, why did I make that decision?

Well, my role was abolished, but despite this I was told in no uncertain terms that I was not a candidate for a redundancy package. Instead, a position would be found for me. It was, but it wasn't what I wanted; also, to be transparent, I was bored and unfulfilled.

So, I decided to catapult myself into the job market and see if I really was as good as people had been telling me I was. (Hello imposter syndrome, I didn't recognise you!) I also felt that if I didn't leave Telstra, I would likely be there for at least another five years, which I believed would make me less employable by outside firms as I could be perceived as 'institutionalised'.

In hindsight, it was a completely bonkers financial decision. Luckily for me, it all worked out.

Now, how does this relate to SQ? Well, I was very quickly hired by one of my former industry partners (a supplier) in a client manager role, which meant, among other things, I needed to effectively build and leverage strategic relationships to fuel the organisation's growth. That meant I needed to network.

I found networking loathsome, and, being transparent again, I was pretty snobby about it. I thought networking was for slimy sales managers to exchange business cards and follow up endlessly with annoying sales calls. Hmm, time for a mindset shift, right? Right!

A few events unfolded, which I'll expand on in later chapters, but to cut a long story short, I came to some realisations:

- Nobody was going to do business with me. I had almost no business networks outside Telstra, nobody in my new industry knew me at all, and my skills and talent gained during my 15 years at Telstra were invisible.
- My boss expected me to have and leverage strategic networks to drive growth. If I wasn't able to do this, then I would probably end up without a job.

So, I decided to learn how to position myself in the industry as an expert in my field who was respected for her ethical approach to business and a trustworthy person to do business with. SQ means that in a crowded and noisy world, you are intentional about building and nurturing your professional brand, and building and leveraging strategic networks.

In Chapter 7: Be Your Own CEO and Chapter 8: Speak Up and Stand Out!, I discuss why brand management and self-promotion is important for success in leadership. Building and maintaining a positive reputation as a leader is incredibly important because, as I discovered painfully, it can significantly impact your ability to influence others, build trust, and achieve career and business goals.

Then I move to one of my favourite subjects in Chapter 9: How to Network Like a CEO. You'll learn how I went from zero to hero in networking, whether in person, online or on social media. I share my stories and techniques for building the confidence to network like a boss (hint: networking *is* working) and leverage your professional brand (hint: your brand is what people say about you when you're not in the room). Both are critical for career and business success.

The discussion around SQ in this book builds on and leverages the prior chapters on EQ and BQ. It completes the explanation of my three leadership skill domains and the range of competencies under each heading.

The Advancing Women Formula

Having well-developed BQ, EQ and SQ positions a woman for a career that soars. It's important to note that leaders with these combined skills are highly valued in modern organisations. In fact, let me be absolutely clear about my opinion on this: the most sought-after people in 21st-century organisations will be those who are known as being able to move organisations forward and manage themselves and others effectively through their expert, ethical and trustworthy approach to business.

This combination of skills and competencies is the secret sauce or magical formula for leadership and career success. It is the Advancing Women Formula.

This book is designed to inform you about the Advancing Women Formula, and provide you with the reasons why each component of the Formula is important and the steps to take to ensure that you enhance and apply these critical business skills, no matter your career stage or the role you occupy in your organisation. Organisational leaders of all genders should find the Advancing Women Formula very helpful to audit their current training and development curriculum for the women in their talent pipeline, as the development experiences generally offered to women – in my opinion and based on my experience auditing those programs – do not focus on BQ or link the competencies associated with EQ and SQ overtly enough to move the organisation forward.

The Advancing Women Formula, with its emphasis on BQ, EQ and SQ, is not just a theoretical concept that I have developed; it is a practical blueprint for women to excel in leadership roles based on my experience and expertise, and the expertise of other very credible people. This book equips women with the knowledge and strategies to develop these skills, which are crucial for navigating the complexities of modern business environments and overcoming the barriers that women still face in advancing their careers and reaching their full potential. Furthermore, it serves as a valuable resource for organisational leaders to ensure they are adequately and effectively preparing women for leadership, thus creating a more equitable, diverse and sustainably successful organisation. The integration of BQ, EQ and SQ is a transformative journey towards exemplary leadership and career advancement.

Chapter 1

Who Are You Called to Become?

My entire life, people have described me as a natural leader. However, I really did not pay much attention to that description; I just happily assumed my mantle of leadership and cracked on with my career. But once my career had advanced to the executive level, I had an opportunity to stop, breathe and reflect on that notion. How did I come to be this way? Why have others characterised me as a leader, especially when I didn't feel leader-like?

The opportunity to ponder this question occurred when I was enrolled in an executive leadership retreat by my employer in 2013. I was among a group of 20 newly appointed executives, and we were some of the most senior 200 executives in an organisation with roughly 30,000 employees. This retreat was designed as our induction into executive leadership at the organisation and aimed to be a transformational experience.

As a fan of leadership development experiences, I was delighted to attend. As a woman fiercely determined to have a successful career, it was a serious marker of success for me. Fair to say, I turned up to the retreat as happy as a dog with ten tails!

The first session at the retreat set the tone for a transformational experience for me. Each of the participants was asked to draw a card at random from a stack at the front of the room. Each card had a unique statement or question on it. We were asked to consider the statement or question and then use it to guide us through an icebreaker networking activity. I happily did this.

But that wasn't the end of it. We were also asked to use the statement or question as a tool to reflect on our leadership story and philosophy, which we were required to document as part of the retreat's outputs. Laughably, I thought that with my typical efficient, task-oriented, process-driven mindset, I could do this reflection business in a couple of hours, knock out a nifty leadership philosophy and that would be that. I'd be top of the class and continue my brilliant career. But the reality was that each time I read the question, my inner coach became louder and more insistent, and I started to question many of the things that formed the status quo in my life.

What was this question that changed my life? It was simply, 'Who are you called to become?'

The question was so powerful because, for decades, I'd had a niggling inner voice that kept reminding me I was 'meant' to do something with my life. I had no idea what the something was, other than that it wasn't what I was doing, even though I loved leadership and had advanced in my career. It puzzled me, but I often ignored this inner voice. Of course, when I felt less happy about my current circumstances, the voice became much more insistent.

Of course, I now know that this inner voice (or my inner coach) was asking me to stop, breathe and reflect. It was begging me to consider where I was and what had brought me there, what still served me and what no longer served me.

So, at the retreat, my inner coach finally had some external help – or maybe I was just ready – and I stopped. I considered the following:

· How did I come to be this way?
· What were the experiences in my life that formed and shaped me?

16

- Who were the people who influenced me?
- What did I need to stop doing, start doing and continue doing?
- Who am I called to become?

This experience, and my commitment to lifelong learning and being open to professional development experiences, have shaped who I am today.

So, who am I called to become?

I am called to become a leader who enables women and organisations to reach their full potential. I am called to become a leader who will help to close the global leadership gender gap. I am called to become a leader who will level the playing field for women and girls.

I took time, and continue to this day, to ask and answer the question of who I am called to become. By reading my book and utilising all the resources you can find at michelleredfern.com/thank-you-for-purchasing-my-book, you will come to understand who you are called to become and that you, too, can navigate successfully and more rapidly towards leadership and reach your full potential.

There are three types of people in the world

I have had the luck and the privilege to report to some terrific leaders throughout my career. In this section, I'm pleased to share the wisdom I gained from them, including some that helped to shape my views about the way I approached leadership early in my senior management career.

In the late 1990s, I was promoted from a sales team manager to an acting contact centre manager. If my memory serves me correctly, I was in the role for somewhere between three and six months. During that period of higher duties, I received advice from my boss (who was a regional general manager) that formed and shaped my perspective on life and leadership.

In 1997, Telstra ceased to be a wholly government-owned entity and became a for-profit corporation listed on the Australian Securities Exchange (ASX). The division I worked in was Consumer Western Australia, and our region was responsible for all of Telstra's non-business sales and customer service in Western Australia. My boss headed up the region and had a leadership team of six people. Each of us was responsible for a large contact centre of hundreds of people.

The leadership team had gathered for an offsite planning session. It was an exciting time for me because, as you'll learn, I was an ambitious and driven leader who put her hand up for anything and everything that would improve my knowledge and skills. So, this was my first opportunity to learn about strategy development from senior leaders I respected.

The offsite went well and I was contributing appropriately given my relatively junior status. In the language we use today, I probably suffered from a combination of imposter syndrome and being a bit starstruck.

At the end of the first day, my boss gave us all a card and a gift. He asked us to open them in private, think about both and then come back to him for a chat. I scurried back to my hotel room and eagerly opened both of mine. The gift was a beautiful silver double-photo frame. A generous gift!

In the card, he had written:

Dear Michelle,

There are three types of people in this world.

People who make things happen.
People who watch things happen.
People who wonder what happened.

Never forget that you are a Type 1 person, and keep making things happen. Thanks for being part of the team.

I initially felt terrific about that. After all, I am a get-shit-done woman! But then I stopped to think. On day one of the offsite, had I behaved as a Type 1, Type 2 or Type 3 person? Yikes! OK, time to get some feedback.

Sure enough, the boss was expecting the question when I cornered him after dinner. He had also anticipated before the offsite that I would be adjusting to my new role as a senior leader, now a peer to the people who used to be my bosses. So, he thoughtfully reminded me why I was part of his team (a Type 1 person) and that despite being starstruck and unsure of myself, I had to step up and be a meaningful contributor to shaping our strategy to win. He also reminded me that work is not life, and that balance and context are essential for great leaders. The photo frame was for me to have a picture of my two children on my desk to be reminded of this daily.

I've learned so much from that boss's wise advice, and it's helped shape my life and leadership style. I delve deeper into this later in the book. I share many practical tips and techniques I've found effective for leading yourself and others towards mutual success.

I am not fixing women (and nor should you)

This book aims to help women navigate the system of work while also advocating for systemic change. I want it to be clear that I have no desire to make women feel like they needed to be fixed. They do not. The system needs fixing. The patriarchal system created by men essentially maintains workplaces, policies, processes and leadership frameworks designed for men.

The idea of not fixing women first came onto my radar when Catherine Fox AM wrote her book *Stop Fixing Women: Why building fairer workplaces is everyone's business*. In the book, Fox points out that women are told a lot about how to be more assertive, be more confident, back themselves more and be more of just about everything! All this advice creates a view for women and the people who lead them that it's women who need fixing, not the system.

When I left the corporate world in 2016, I was clear that I wanted to help women ascend more rapidly into leadership roles and reach their full potential. However, I was also aware that working directly with women to build their skills, capability and capacity was just part of the equation of advancing women's success. The other critical component is working with the organisations where women work to fix their systems of work that result in a widely yawning gender gap in leadership.

My friend, colleague and strategic mentor Susan Colantuono helped refine my thinking about a system-wide approach to advancing women. She told me that providing women in organisations with access to leadership development programs, as we are doing, is terrific. However, organisational leaders must also take action to address the barriers to career advancement that women face in their organisations. Failure to do so results in a pipeline of talented but very frustrated women who continue to bang their heads against the glass ceiling.

So, this book is an extension of my desire to be like a human compass for women. In plain English, I want to fix the system that is still fundamentally stacked against women. However, I also want to help women successfully navigate the system, using my decades of leadership experience across a range of industries as well as my nearly a decade of work advocating and creating solutions for workplace gender equity.

A component of my 'compass service' is this book, which aims not to fix women but to provide women (and their employers) with access to knowledge, wisdom and facts about the steps they can take to maximise their advancement opportunities.

The facts about women in leadership

The global leadership gender gap must be closed, and women must be given the same career and earning opportunities and success as men.

Women comprise more than half of the world's population and roughly 42% of all (paid) working people, but they experience higher unemployment rates than men and experience substandard working conditions more often than men. They also hold only a fraction of leadership positions (see figure 1.1).

Figure 1.1: The global leadership gender gap

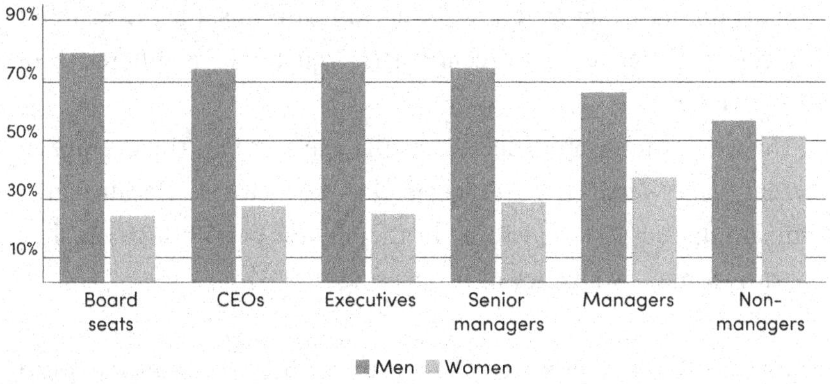

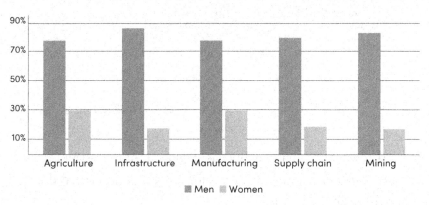

SOURCE: CATALYST

Figure 1.2 shows that women are outnumbered by men in leadership positions particularly in industries such as agriculture, infrastructure, manufacturing, supply chain and mining, where the representation of women in senior leadership is as low as 16%.

Figure 1.2: Women's representation in senior leadership

SOURCE: LINKEDIN'S ECONOMIC GRAPH

Globally, women earn just 83 cents for every dollar men earn. The gender pay gap is wider for women of colour (58 cents) and women from other marginalised communities. Even when women make it to senior management roles, the difference between women's and men's pay is 11%. In my home country of Australia, the gender pay gap, which organisations with over 100 full-time employees are legislated to report on, has stagnated at 13%; or, in real terms, for every dollar men earn, women earn 87 cents. That equates to a difference of $13,119.60 per year.

The gender pay gap is defined as the gap between the average of all men's wages versus the average of all women's wages. Because men dominate the highest paid roles, in the highest paid industries, they out-earn women by a factor of two (see figure 1.3).

Figure 1.3: Men are twice as likely than women to be highly paid

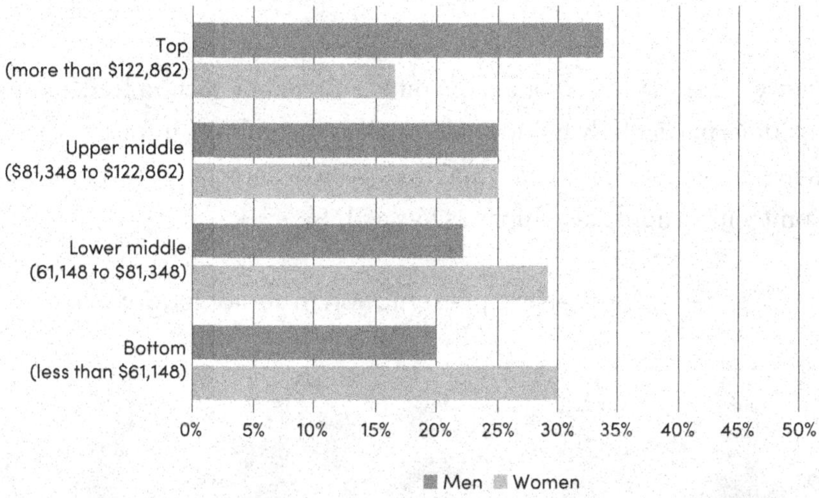

SOURCE: *AUSTRALIA'S GENDER EQUALITY SCORECARD* (2022)

Progress towards gender equality has stagnated. At the current rate of change, it will take another 135 years for the gap to close, according to the World Economic Forum.

The leaky talent pipeline and the resulting career and earning inequity for women will not be fixed in my lifetime unless deliberate, urgent action is undertaken.

Closing the leadership gender gap requires all of us, but particularly those of us who have talent management responsibility (that is, organisational leaders), to understand the three major causes:

1. **The system.** Policies and practices (or their absence) can adversely impact women's advancement to senior or executive positions.
2. **Managers' mindsets.** Unexamined mindsets about women and leadership mean managers are making potentially biased talent decisions.
3. **Women's skill sets.** Women must demonstrate the critical skills required for advancement into senior and executive positions.

Closing the global leadership gender gap will require a concerted effort from individuals, organisations and governments to address all three causes:

-   **Individual women** can take steps to develop and demonstrate their business, strategic and financial acumen, and they must advocate for themselves to receive coaching, mentoring and development that matters.
-   **Organisations** must create more inclusive workplaces that support women's advancement. Developing and implementing a workplace gender equity strategy that includes building diversity, equity and inclusion (DEI) accountability and skill sets in leaders is the minimum level of action required.
-   **Governments** must legislate for workplace gender equity. Legislation must include minimum standards for promoting and improving workplace gender equity.

The global leadership gender gap is a complex problem we can all resolve. Working individually and collectively, we can create a more equitable world where women have the same opportunities to lead as men.

What is (still) missing for women at work?

Achieving career success – and all the benefits that come with that – requires women, their employers, their coaches and mentors, and learning professionals to pay (more) attention to the critical skill sets that women must develop and demonstrate to be considered for advancement.

Let me explain two critical facts about career advancement:

1. Business intelligence (BQ) plus emotional intelligence (EQ) plus social intelligence (SQ) equals higher leadership positions.
2. BQ is often the missing link in the career success formula for women.

BQ is the missing link because even though 50% of the selection criteria for senior roles relates to business skills, less than 3% of the career advice, coaching, mentoring, conferences and literature aimed at women includes this critical content, according to the responses I've received from programs and workshops I have facilitated since 2016.

I recently surveyed 50 women in middle management at an ASX-listed company. The women were participating in a leadership program I was running. I asked them, 'What is the best career advice you have ever received?' and 98% of the women told me that their best career advice had nothing to do with building and demonstrating their business skills.

While people and social networking skills are essential, the leadership equation is incomplete without an understanding of how to run a business successfully and sustainably. Still, not enough women are being given the career advice, mentoring, coaching or training in the leadership competencies required to ascend to the most senior levels. Material developed for women still over-indexes on confidence, assertiveness and self-advocacy content. Women must be effectively coached, mentored and trained to be senior leaders.

So, this book is unashamedly designed to enable women to acquire and showcase all the skills necessary for career advancement.

Go deeper

Each chapter of this book has a 'Go deeper' section, providing you, the reader, with a range of extension tasks and downloadable activities to further enhance your leadership skills.

Take the time to read each chapter and complete the activities (including the reflection and feedback activities!) to develop the skills you need in each area systematically. Many of the activities can be shared with your team members and colleagues, and used as team capability-building exercises, in coaching discussions with your boss and in mentoring discussions with your mentor.

In addition, I highly recommend you join the Lead to Soar Network, listen to the *Lead to Soar* podcast and attend our annual Lead to Soar Summits in Australia and the USA so you can continue to learn from me, Susan Colantuono, Mel Butcher (a co-host of *Lead to Soar*) and hundreds of other ambitious, driven women leaders like you:

Lead to Soar Network	*Lead to Soar* podcast
leadtosoar.network/plans	shows.acast.com/lead-to-soar

Chapter 2

Leadership that Gets Results

If you have ever read a book about business, most likely it was authored by a man. *Fortune* magazine published an article in 2020 titled 'Men Named Jo(h)n Have Written as Many of 2020's Top Business Books as All Women Combined'. The report also claims that of the top 200 best-selling business books, just 17 were written by women.

I do find it extraordinarily ironic that publishers continue to favour old white guys to write pretty much anything about business, yet when it comes to corporate and business scandals, that same demographic features heavily among the architects. Think of Enron, FIFA, Volkswagen, the sub-prime scandal and the global financial crisis.

Of course, it makes sense that men feature more heavily than women in these scandals because men have dominated the C-suite since the dawn of the C-suite. Someone once told me that she will be satisfied we have achieved gender equality when there are as many incompetent women as leaders as men.

Why am I sharing this? Because old white guys do not have a monopoly on good ideas and the writing of good business books.

When women read books by the usual suspects – that is, the 183 male authors in 2020 – about how to be good in business, run a good business and be a great leader or CEO, they are receiving conventional leadership advice from a very homogenous group of people with arguably similar lived experiences, mindsets and attributes. Only reading books authored by men means neglecting the views and unmet needs of over half of the world's population.

My life's mission is to close the global leadership gender gap. Every woman in the world who is interested in business must diversify their sources of information to gain a more comprehensive perspective on business and life.

Therefore, one of the many reasons I am writing this book is to offer women business skills-building advice from a woman's perspective. As well as drawing from my own experience of a successful corporate career, a board director portfolio and running a small business, I have also enlisted other accomplished women, including successful CEOs, entrepreneurs and senior sports administrators, to share their experiences and advice so we can learn from their wisdom. I advise all women navigating their careers to learn from those who came before them, regardless of gender.

I'd like you to imagine for a moment that you could talk with the CEO of your current company for an hour. What would you ask them? Well, I have asked successful women CEOs from various sectors to help you understand what CEOs want you to know; their advice features throughout the book.

Nickie Scriven is a highly accomplished CEO in the marketing and advertising industry. She is also an entrepreneur who has founded two businesses and is a board director in the sports sector. When I asked Nickie for advice on how women can progress in their careers, she offered the following:

'Start thinking about the positive impact you can have on the organisation to drive growth. Think strategically rather than operationally. To move into leadership, you need to lead, not operate, so you need to start thinking strategically about what and how you can lead and make a positive impact. Middle management is usually quite operational. To step up, you need to get out of the weeds and stand on the balcony to see what's ahead and chart the path forward.'

I wholeheartedly agree with Nickie, and so in this chapter I break down three key themes in what Nickie has shared to outline what leadership that gets results looks like and how to do more of it:

1. Drive growth.
2. Think strategically.
3. Lead, don't just operate.

Drive growth

Successful leaders have a clear and concise plan for their company's future and try to achieve it through commitment and persistence. Leaders at every career stage need to be able to continuously scan for opportunities to drive growth and ensure they work towards that growth efficiently and effectively. Put simply, you must look for opportunities to get the right stuff done at the right time with the right people.

Being known as a growth leader means being acutely aware of how your organisation intends to grow and prioritising your activities to support that. Organisations grow through a combination of strategies and activities:

· **Market penetration** or organic customer growth involves selling more existing products or services to the existing customer base. It may include increasing marketing efforts, offering promotions or discounts, or enhancing the product or service to encourage higher consumption – or, as it is sometimes known, 'greater share of customer wallet'.

- **Market development** involves entering new markets, either geographically or demographically. For example, an organisation that has succeeded in one country may expand its operations to another, or it may choose to try to attract and retain gen Z or millennial buyers when the existing products and services are targeted at gen X or baby boomers.

- **Product development** involves developing new products or services to serve existing or new markets. It may involve innovation, research and development to create new offerings that meet customers' changing needs and preferences. It is risky when organisations develop new products to expand their customer base because this involves two unknowns: new products and new markets.

- **Acquisitions and mergers** with other companies can provide quick access to new markets, products or technologies. It can also lead to cost savings through economies of scale, as the acquired business can leverage the centralised or shared services of the acquirer to reduce costs and increase the effectiveness of operational and customer-facing divisions.

- **Strategic partnerships and alliances** with other organisations can provide access to new customers, technologies or resources without needing a full merger or acquisition. There is lot of work and risk associated with mergers and acquisitions, not least of which includes the loss of productivity while the merger or acquisition is underway, so strategic alliances can make sense to create competitive advantage.

- **Cost management** opens up choices. By becoming the most cost-effective producer in the market, an organisation can offer lower prices to its customers, thereby increasing its market share and/or profits that can be directed towards further growth strategies.

However, it's important not to neglect your existing customers in pursuit of growth. Retaining existing customers is often much more cost-effective than acquiring new ones and prevents you from undoing the growth you can achieve through these strategies and activities.

Yes, you are a growth leader

Whether you're at the start of your career, in middle or senior management, or already at the executive or C-suite level, you have a responsibility to drive growth. One of the many things that Susan Colantuono has taught me is that 'leadership manifests itself at every level, in every organisation'. However, that responsibility is different depending on where you are. So, different ways of driving growth in your organisation will be available to you depending on your career stage.

Here's how you can drive growth in your organisation at the start of your career:

- Develop a clear understanding of your organisation's growth strategy and how your role and team contribute to achieving it.
- Become an expert in your field and continuously update your skills so you can contribute ideas and expertise.
- Collaborate with others by sharing knowledge and insights.
- Nail your KPIs (key performance indicators) because they will be linked to the organisational growth strategy.

From middle or senior management, you can drive growth by undertaking all of the actions in the previous list, plus the following:

- **Translate strategy into action.** You're the glue between the executives, who create the strategic growth plans for the organisation, and your team members, who execute those plans. Use your excellent communication skills to synthesise and translate the strategic objectives into actionable growth plans for your teams.
- **Manage people.** (It sort of goes without saying but I'm going to say it anyway!) To achieve growth targets, you need to make

sure that you have the right people in the right places doing the right things in the right way. That means recruiting, training, developing and performance-managing folks in your teams.

- **Innovate and continuously improve.** You have access to your frontline team members in operations and customer roles, which positions you to continuously scan for improved ways of working and growing, and funnel those ideas to executives.

- **Ensure customer satisfaction.** Happy customers are key to growth, and you play a crucial role in ensuring that your organisation meets or exceeds customers' expectations.

- **Monitor and report.** What gets measured gets managed, and it's part of your role to monitor the performance of your teams and report on performance. This includes identifying and addressing any issues or challenges that may be hindering growth and proposing solutions to address them.

At the executive or C-suite level, you can drive growth by undertaking all of the actions in the previous two lists, plus the following:

- **Set the overall vision and strategic direction of the organisation.** When you're at the top of an organisation, you and your colleagues identify opportunities for growth, define the organisation's goals and develop strategies to achieve those goals.

- **Allocate resources.** This is about making sure you have the right things in the right places at the right time. You're responsible for ensuring that the enablers of growth – including finances, personnel and technology – are all lined up to support the growth strategy. This includes making decisions about investments, acquisitions and partnerships or alliances, as well as about entering new markets and developing new products or services. It also means having a robust talent management strategy.

- **Build a strong culture.** This should not be news to you, but it's worth emphasising (especially given what I've already shared about organisational scandals) that the C-suite sets the tone for the organisation's culture. An ethical, inclusive and positive culture that encourages innovation, collaboration and continuous improvement is essential for sustainable growth.

· **Build strong relationships with stakeholders outside of the organisation.** This is a hallmark of the executive's role; the more senior your role, the greater the importance of this external relationship management. Relationships with investors, customers, suppliers, governments and regulators are the domain of the executive and are enablers of, or barriers to, growth.

· **Identify, manage and mitigate risks that could impact the organisation's growth.** These include external threats, such as market or regulatory environment changes, and internal threats, such as operational or financial risks.

When I asked Carol-Ann Gough, Chief Information Officer of Great Southern Bank in Australia, about what game-changing leadership is, she said, 'Create environments that energise and empower people, teams and leaders to solve challenging problems, embrace opportunities and grow in ways they never expected or thought possible'.

This sums up what it takes to be a growth leader well. No matter your career stage, yes, you are a growth leader!

Think strategically

I asked CEO, board chair and director Helga Svendsen to define strategy. She explained that strategy cannot be easily defined with just one sentence; it is unique to each organisation and varies depending on where the organisation is in its lifecycle. For example, the strategy for a start-up will differ to that of a growing organisation, which will differ to that of a mature organisation or an organisation that is undergoing liquidation. There is no universal strategy that fits every organisation. Finding the right strategy for your organisation involves looking ahead and taking a step back to evaluate the bigger picture.

In a 2007 *Harvard Business Review* article, Michael D Watkins wrote, 'A good strategy provides a clear roadmap, consisting of a set of guiding principles or rules, that defines the actions people in the business should take (and not take) and the things they should prioritize (and not prioritize) to achieve desired goals.'

Just as you can be a growth leader at any level, you can also be a strategic leader at any level. However, which strategy you focus on depends on which career stage you are at (see table 2.1).

Table 2.1: Strategy focuses at different career stages

Career stage	Strategy focus
Career start	Personal strategy: Ensure that you are achieving your KPIs, which contribute to the team strategy.
Middle to senior management	Team strategy: Ensure that the day-to-day activities of the team are moving the organisation in the right direction to achieve its overarching goals.
Executive to C-suite	Corporate strategy: Develop and implement a strategy to support the vision and mission of the organisation. Business unit strategy: Develop a strategy to determine how the business units will compete in their various markets.

Developing strategy

A 2022 McKinsey article described the CEO as not only 'the company's ultimate strategist' but 'also the ultimate integrator', with the task of identifying and responding to enterprise-spanning issues. 'To do that well requires a broad range of contradictory perspectives: outside in and inside out, a telescope to see the world and a microscope to break it down, a snapshot view of the immediate issues and a time-lapse series to see into the future.'

However, as discussed, strategy development can be undertaken at every career stage. The simple process of developing a strategy is to:

1. analyse the past and the present
2. anticipate future trends and needs
3. forecast how the business will perform in predicted conditions
4. prepare people and the organisation to respond to these findings.

As a businesswoman, you must possess a comprehensive understanding of your organisation's overall vision, strategic pillars, and strategy development and review cycles, as well as the specific steps and timeline to implement each strategy. An organisation's strategic pillars are the four to six major goals that will deliver its vision and mission. For example, Telstra, Australia's largest ASX-listed telecommunications company, lists its strategic pillars on page 10 of its 2023 annual report:

'1. Provide an exceptional customer experience you can count on
2. Provide leading network and technology solutions that deliver your future
3. Create sustained growth and value for our shareholders
4. Be the place [where] you want to work.'

Understanding your firm's strategic pillars is important. It is equally important that you know what your responsibilities are for contributing to the organisation delivering on these promises to stakeholders.

How to be more strategic

I have repeatedly heard two things when it comes to strategy and women over the course of my career. First, women are consistently given the feedback that they must 'be more strategic' to advance their careers. Sigh. While I have no issue with the suggestion that women develop their strategic acumen, please, leaders, take the time to help them understand what you think 'being more strategic' looks and sounds like.

Second, many women I have spoken to about their career aspirations have expressed a strong desire to 'get into strategy'. However, it's important to understand that we all engage in strategic thinking, regardless of our job titles or departmental structures. While some companies may have dedicated strategy departments, there are plenty of opportunities to cultivate and showcase strategic thinking skills:

- **Understand the big picture.** Remember to read your organisation's annual, half-yearly and quarterly business reports and any releases to the investor or stakeholder community. Analyse the industry, market trends, customer trends and geopolitical situation for opportunities and risks to you and your organisation. Ask yourself what the most important strategic imperative is that your CEO and board of directors want you to know about and accomplish.

- **Foster your curiosity.** Broaden your reading list to include business and industry publications. Hang out with people 'in the know' at your organisation or in your industry and ask them questions about the future. Attend webinars, seminars and conferences that expose you to strategic thinking and thinkers. Ask your manager and senior management questions about the direction your organisation is taking and why: What are we here to do? What's the problem we are trying to solve? What is the future we want to see? What are the values that support that vision?

- **Pursue development opportunities.** Cross-functional project teams allow you to learn about different parts of your organisation, reducing siloed thinking. Also, seek a mentor with the strategic skills and track record to help you develop your strategic thinking.

Being strategic means taking the initiative and making decisions that set up your organisation for success in the long run. It's crucial to demonstrate your expertise and establish yourself as a knowledgeable and strategic businesswoman.

One frustration CEOs have is that there is a gap between strategy and performance, and just 63% of strategic initiatives translate to a lift in financial performance. Demonstrating that you are a business-woman who is 'in the know', understands 'the big picture' and can close the strategy-to-performance gap means, according to Carol-Ann Gough, 'taking people and teams from a siloed approach or mindset to an enterprise or wider-system mindset so they see the value of their work, have a greater impact on business performance, inspire and motivate others, and grow their capability to be "ready for next"'.

There are several practical steps you can take to showcase your strategic acumen:

· Include a standing agenda item for your team meetings to discuss industry trends, customer dynamics and external factors that could impact your organisation. (Ask your boss to do this as well!)

· If you work in a publicly listed or traded organisation, keep an eye on the share price and what is driving its fluctuations. Discuss the share price and earnings-per-share (EPS) performance, and the drivers, with your manager in one-on-ones and coaching sessions, and ask questions.

· Ensure that you understand what Susan Colantuono calls your 'positional purpose' (which I discuss further in the next section) and how your role contributes to the organisation's strategic and financial goals. Check out the strategic mapping exercise in her book *No Ceiling, No Walls* to help you with this.

· Speak up about how you and your team can contribute to the organisation's strategy accomplishment. Make suggestions for improvements in the business that are aligned to the strategy.

· Prioritise your tasks by analysing what occupies most of your time and assessing if it is aligned with your organisation's mission.

It's sadly very easy to get 'busy', but are you busy with the most important thing to move the organisation forward?

· Track your performance, and your team's performance, against the organisation's long-term plans. Then, prioritise closing performance gaps and leveraging performance strengths.

· If you are a team leader, ensure you have the right people in the right place doing the right things at the right time. Inadequate or misdirected resources are a sure-fire way to create performance gaps.

· To showcase your interest in the company's strategic direction, talk with your boss about your role and how it fits into the bigger picture. This will help shape your manager's perception of you as a person who is focused on strategy.

Helga Svendsen advises:

'Know what the vision and the purpose of the organisation is, know what those chunks of work are, and know where you fit into that. If you can't see that, ask your boss. You can say, "I've got the strategy here, boss, and I can see the vision and the pillar for this. I think I fit in here. But I would love to have a conversation with you about the work that I do and how our team fits into the big-picture strategy of this organisation. I'd love to be able to understand that so I can make my contribution. Could we have a conversation about it?"'

Lead, don't just operate

The third enabler of leadership greatness is to lead, not just operate. What does that mean? It means to work on the business, not just in the business. To get off the dance floor and onto the balcony. To get out of the weeds, and to see the wood, not just the trees.

To be a leader rather than just a worker, it's important to pause, take a breath and consider how you can positively impact your organisation. This involves ensuring that you are fulfilling your positional purpose. What is your role in the company? What are your specific responsibilities and goals? What do you do daily to help achieve the organisation's objectives? These are the important things to consider when considering how your position within the organisation can have the greatest positive impact.

Imagine you are the captain of a cruise liner. You have passengers (customers) who depend on you for a great time on their holiday. The cruise ship organisation depends on you to ensure customers have a great experience so they become repeat customers. Your crew depend on you to ensure the working environment is safe and respectful, and that they have all the tools and resources to get their job done.

As the captain, you're working from the bridge, and in front of you is the large dashboard that tells you where the ship is headed and how it is performing. You have executive team members who report to you to tell you how the customer experience is going and how the crew are performing.

Now, imagine if you spent the entire cruise down in the engine room focusing on the mechanical aspects of the ship, fixing up the day-to-day, tactical performance issues that arise from time to time. You're good at this work because it's your original area of technical expertise, and your high performance and expertise in this area is how you progressed to senior roles in the company. But you're missing out on the perspective you'd get on the bridge, watching out for the overall performance of the cruise liner and all the people on it.

It wouldn't happen, would it? The cruise liner captain, who is responsible for thousands of people's lives and the organisation's reputation, wouldn't stay below deck tinkering with the engines for the entire cruise. Sure, they might visit the engine room from time to time to check in, but they would know when to get out again and lead the cruise liner towards its goal.

What about you? How are you leading your part of the organisation? Are you on the bridge or down in the engine room? Are you focused on your organisation's strategic and financial goals and your responsibility to deliver outcomes that contribute towards those goals? Or are you constantly stuck in the weeds, tinkering with the day-to-day operational details?

To progress successfully from individual contributor to frontline manager, then to middle and senior management and finally into executive and C-suite roles, you must learn to lift your eyes to the next level, check for internal and external threats and opportunities, and chart the path forward. You won't be able to do that from the engine room.

Stop, breathe, reflect

Lifting your eyes to the next level must be a deliberate, intentional act. And, as a leader, it's important to lead by example and inspire others to follow in your footsteps.

I remember an executive in the division that I worked in at Telstra who would take a break every afternoon to gaze out the window for 30 minutes to an hour. Initially, I was unsure about this behaviour, but after checking in with my boss I was informed that the executive was using this time to think and plan. He was trying to make sense of things and develop fresh ideas to move the business forward. Although I didn't realise it then, this was an important lesson in leadership.

We cannot keep trudging through our daily tasks like lemmings approaching a cliff edge, or hurtling about like hamsters on a wheel. Whether we're inexorably putting one foot in front of the other each week or running fast, being busy but not stopping to reflect on whether we're still headed in the right direction or working on the right stuff is fundamentally flawed behaviour. Effective leaders set aside time for self-reflection. They evaluate their current performance and determine what actions they need to focus on or dial back to continually improve.

I'd like you to do that right now. What are your planned activities for the next day, week or month? Are they related to the outcomes you have to deliver in your role for your team or your business? If not, then it is time to reprioritise.

These activities include the meetings you plan to attend or have been invited to. I want $10 for every time I have heard women say that they have been in back-to-back meetings all day or week, or that they have been too busy to undertake important self-development activities such as courses, conferences or strategic networking.

Effective leaders run their days; they do not let their days run them. So, I do not want you to turn up to every meeting you are invited to. I want you to question whether you need to be there or whether someone else could be your delegate – or, as is the case too often, whether the purpose of the meeting could be solved with a well-worded email.

Look at your calendars, leaders. I want you to follow the practice of that executive at Telstra, as I have done diligently for more than 15 years now, and block out time for reflection, problem-solving or professional development – preferably, all three. If you're feeling a little reluctant to do that, consider this quote:

> 'Instead of saying "I don't have time" try saying "It's not a priority" and see how that feels. "I'm not working on my growth because it's not a priority." If it doesn't sit well, that's the point. Time is a choice. If we don't like how we're spending it, we can choose differently.'

A word or two about busyness

I used to wear being busy as a badge of honour. Being frantically busy was a great big ego trip for me because it showed everyone how important I was. *I have to go to all these meetings, answer all those emails, busy, busy, busy!* What utter bullshit!

You know what? Despite all that busyness, I didn't know if I was focusing on the right things. How could I? I never took time out to stop, breathe and reflect on where I was, how I got there and where I needed to go next.

Please, let's stop saying we're busy. If you're 'busy' all the time, rushing from meeting to meeting and dashing off emails at ridiculous times of the night or over the weekend (yes, this is autobiographical!), this is detracting from the perception of you as a leader who is approachable and can contribute to organisational outcomes.

Please ensure that you block out time in your diary for things that will position you for success in your current role and in your next role, such as driving growth, thinking and acting strategically, and planning. These things will not magically fit themselves in around everything else. You need to prioritise activities that align with your positional purpose.

Finally, if you do get an opportunity to talk with your organisation's CEO, an executive or your boss's boss, ask them these three questions:

1. What are the top three issues that keep you awake at night?
2. What would you like me to do more to address those issues?
3. What would you want me to do less to address those issues?

Go deeper

Stop. Breathe. Reflect.

Performing a personal SWOT analysis is a valuable exercise that helps you understand your current career position, potential challenges and growth opportunities. It aims to determine the steps you can take to achieve mastery in your current role or meet the prerequisites for your next big career move.

SWOT stands for:

S = Strengths
W = Weaknesses
O = Opportunities
T = Threats

This process entails considering your inherent (internal) strengths and weaknesses, as well as external opportunities and threats. It is crucial to approach your SWOT analysis as if you are running a business and view yourself as a competitive product. Remember to assess your BQ skills – business, strategic and financial acumen – when you complete your SWOT analysis.

Your personal SWOT analysis is a structured way to help you understand your current position in your career and identify where potential opportunities or challenges might lie. Here's a step-by-step guide to help you create your personal SWOT analysis:

1. **Prepare.** Find a quiet space where you won't be disturbed. Get out a notebook or piece of paper, or use a digital tool. (Some people prefer large sheets of paper or whiteboards for a visual overview.) Divide the paper into four quadrants and label them 'strengths', 'weaknesses', 'opportunities' and 'threats' (see table 2.2).

Table 2.2: Personal SWOT analysis

Strengths	Weaknesses
Examples: Strong communication skills, expertise in specific software, a vast professional network	Examples: Difficulty with public speaking, lack of experience in a particular industry, not being up to date with the latest technological trends
Opportunities	**Threats**
Examples: Upcoming training sessions, networking events, a trend in your industry where your specific skills could be in high demand	Examples: Economic downturns, advancements in technology that could make your skills obsolete, increasing competition in your industry

2. **Consider your strengths.** Reflect on your achievements and what was essential for you to achieve them. List the skills, resources, capabilities and personal qualities you possess. Ask yourself: *What do I excel at? What do others see as my strengths? What unique resources can I draw upon that others might not have? What do I do better than anyone else?*

3. **Consider your weaknesses.** Be honest about the areas where you struggle or need improvement. In what areas do you feel less confident? What tasks do you usually avoid because you don't feel competent? What do others identify as areas for your improvement? Are there gaps in your skill set that need addressing?

4. **Consider your opportunities.** Think about the external factors you can capitalise on. Are there emerging trends in your industry or field? Can you exploit changes in technology or policy, or societal shifts? Are there upcoming events, courses or conferences that could benefit you? Are there gaps in the market or job positions you could fill? Can you leverage your network more effectively?

5. **Consider your threats.** Reflect on external challenges that could harm your career. Are there challenges in your industry that could impact your job? Is the number of roles in your field shrinking, or are jobs being outsourced? Is technology advancing in a way that could make your skills obsolete? Do you have personal limitations that could pose future challenges? Are there financial or geopolitical factors that might affect your career?

6. **Review and reflect.** Look at your SWOT matrix critically. Are there ways you can use your strengths to take advantage of opportunities or mitigate any of the threats? Are there weaknesses you must address so you can exploit potential opportunities or neutralise threats?

7. **Create an action plan.** Think about steps you can take for each of the SWOT elements and convert your findings into a strategy. For instance, if one of your weaknesses is a lack of knowledge about a booming technology, your action might be to take a course on that subject.

8. **Seek feedback.** Sometimes we have blind spots regarding our strengths and weaknesses. Discussing your SWOT analysis with mentors, colleagues, friends or coaches can be beneficial. They might offer insights or perspectives you hadn't considered.

9. **Regularly update your analysis.** Your personal SWOT analysis isn't static; it should evolve as you grow in your career. Make a point to revisit and update your SWOT analysis annually or when you're considering a career change.

Remember, the goal of a SWOT analysis is not just to identify these elements but also to take informed actions to amplify your strengths, address your weaknesses, capitalise on opportunities and guard against threats.

Chapter 3

Metrics that Matter

In late 2004, I was a senior manager in Broadband Field Services, a business unit (BU) in Telstra. I loved the work we did in this BU and I loved my role, which had a dual focus: leading the service centre of around 100 people who organised technical assistance for our broadband internet and cable TV subscription customers; and managing the relationships with our two key customers, the broadband internet provider for Telstra and the external client who provided pay TV services, along with the two outsource partners who supplied all our technical staff. The bonus was that, for the first time in my senior management career, I reported to an executive who was a woman. Her name was Debbie Nankivell, and her leadership style and approach greatly impacted my leadership development.

I had been in the role for around 18 months when we learned that our BU was being shut down and subsumed into other areas of Telstra. I was no stranger to change, and having been at Telstra for nearly 15 years and working in two states of Australia in three different divisions, I had seen my fair share of organisational restructures. I also knew that reorganising the business was necessary to maintain a competitive edge. But this one hurt. I loved the work we were doing, and despite the usual challenges of leading a large, diverse team of people inside and outside the organisation, it was interesting. I loved my role. I also formed very strong relationships with my colleagues, some of whom had been in this BU for a long time. Having the responsibility to announce the change and why it was happening (which I disagreed with) and then tell people how their work lives would change substantially was emotionally taxing for me. I also had the stress of not knowing what was next for me, as I knew up-front that my role would no longer exist and I would be redeployed (no redundancy payout for me!), and it was still a mystery where I would be redeployed to.

The months rolled on and the restructuring project (which I was a lead on) concluded, and I found myself considering my future. I was a 15-year veteran of Telstra. I had been redeployed into a job that had been created for me, and while I was grateful, I didn't want the role; I had no passion for it and couldn't see any future in it. I asked to be made redundant again and was told in no uncertain terms that my (high) performance made that impossible, and that there were 'great plans' for me.

It was May 2005. That month, I visited my home state of Western Australia for my beloved Nana's 90th birthday, and I turned 40. Life milestones often cause me to stop, breathe and reflect. Some may say it was a midlife crisis, but I decided, after discussing it with my amazing partner in life, Rhonda, that I would resign from Telstra and work in the 'real world'. Managers and others had told me for years that I was talented and high-performing and had high potential, but I felt that my career was stalling. So, I decided to take a risk and see if I had what it took to be successful in a business that wasn't Telstra.

It was one of my better decisions. I quickly landed what turned out to be one of the most pivotal roles in my career. It was at an organisation called UCMS, an outsourced call-centre company I was already acquainted with: UCMS was a large provider of call-centre services to Telstra. Before my broadband role, I had been responsible for managing the relationship with, and performance of, UCMS for Telstra. I had a fabulous relationship with the folks at UCMS; we had done great business together.

When I started at UCMS, the Executive General Manager of Client Services was Denice Pitt. She was my two-up manager. Soon after, Denice became our CEO. I was thrilled that a woman was leading our organisation, and especially that it was Denice, who had profoundly impacted my career. I learned from Denice the importance of being known for having business, strategic and financial acumen.

During my first week at UCMS, Denice gave me some of the best career advice ever. She told me that my role working in contact centre outsourcing would be the best general management training I could get. She was right!

The cold, hard, brutal truths

When UCMS hired me as a commercial relationships manager, they assumed I had a certain level of skill and competency. As a result, rather than place me in an operational call-centre role, they asked me to manage current client relationships and grow the business organically through those relationships.

I was then, and still am, very good at managing relationships. I was then, and still am, an extremely commercially minded, business-savvy woman. Except back then, my business savvy was highly instinctual. My new employers hired me for my business, strategic and financial acumen, but I was faking the financial acumen part.

I didn't intentionally set out to fake it. However, when I started executing my responsibilities, I discovered that a pressing priority was to address the financial underperformance of one of our client call centres. At that point, I had to have the strength of character and intestinal fortitude to admit some cold, hard, brutal truths to myself. Despite being an expert in the metrics associated with managing the operations of a call centre, I lacked the essential skills to make this call centre a valuable business unit. Here's why:

- I lacked the skills to understand the current financial model and its link to the current contractual requirements.
- I lacked the skills to develop an alternate pricing model to address the underperformance.
- I could not effectively communicate with and manage the performance of the operational managers who needed to urgently address the call centre's underperformance.
- I did not fully comprehend how the call centre affected the company's financial objectives.

I could not drive better results because I could not effectively diagnose the status quo, did not know the numbers well enough and was not sufficiently aware of the overall goal. This was my first test, post-Telstra, to see if I had what it took to be successful in a highly commercial, competitive business environment.

Time to act

I've told this story because I have heard from women, and still hear too often for my liking, statements like these:

'I'm just not good with numbers.'

'I avoid the numbers because I'm not comfortable with them.'

'Numbers aren't my thing. People are.'

It's important to clarify that 'the numbers' encompasses all relevant metrics in an organisation, which includes financial measurements. Since I spent many of my formative management years in call centres, I was comfortable with many metrics. However, I had not developed the skills to link those metrics to the financial metrics. As a result, when I developed strategies to determine what operational levers to pull to ensure a positive outcome, I was led by instinct rather than overtly identifying and focusing on the strategic and financial goals of the organisation and how I could contribute to them.

So, back to my cold, hard, brutal truths. I admit, I did have a mini-meltdown and spun my wheels for a few days, wondering what on earth I was going to do about this underperforming contract call centre. Then I decided to do two very sensible things.

First, I spilled the beans to Rhonda about my predicament. Rhonda is a finance expert, and she promptly took me in hand and taught me the basics of finance: how to read and manage the profit and loss of the business, understand the budget and link it to the contract. She gave me six months of intensive financial acumen tutoring based on my real-life work. That tutoring continues to this day!

Second, I asked my boss who could best mentor me to improve the financial performance of my contracts. I admitted that I needed someone who both knew the business and could help fast-track my in-depth understanding of the financial systems and processes at UCMS. I was assigned to one of the finance team's management accountants, and he and I would spend an hour or so each month working through the financial results of all my contracts and developing strategies to enhance performance.

I do have financial acumen, but I must work a bit harder at it than, say, my wife, who spends her days mulling over the intricacies of cash flow, balance sheets, profit and loss, and complex financial data. The point here is that I do not ignore my responsibility as a leader, director and business owner to be intentional about continuously improving my financial acumen.

When I was undertaking the corporate finance unit of my MBA, my lecturer said, 'CEOs do not need to understand every global accounting or finance principle in detail. They have a CFO to do that. But they need to be able to ask the right questions, hold people accountable and call bullshit on dodgy stuff!'

The role of a leader is to ensure that the organisation is meeting its strategic and financial goals. Leaders cannot drive positive financial results if they do not know what the financial goals are or how to achieve them. So, it is your responsibility to ensure that you have, and are demonstrating, your financial acumen in your leadership role. I emphasise demonstrating your financial acumen because when you are known as a businesswoman with good financial acumen, you are more likely to be considered for roles with more responsibility and seniority than women who are not viewed as financially savvy.

Financial acumen is not Accounting 101

At its core, financial acumen is the ability to understand and apply financial principles to make better decisions in business. But it goes beyond just understanding financial statements, budgets and forecasts. It also requires an outside perspective (as I discussed in chapter 2), applying your strategic thinking capability by scanning the external environment for economic forces and market trends that can create financial headwinds and tailwinds for your organisation. When leaders combine their strategic thinking with financial acumen, they make better and more informed decisions.

Effective leaders know the numbers and the metrics that matter. Effective leaders know their business and their role in achieving and sustaining the strategic and financial outcomes critical to the organisation's success. Unfortunately, many women I have worked with over the past decade are still not being directly taught that they must know, and be known for knowing, 'the numbers' from the outset of their careers, and coached, mentored and trained in how to do this.

Nickie Scriven told me that she wishes she'd been told earlier in her career to lean into the financials, and really understand profit and loss and financial modelling. Me too!

How to improve your financial acumen

The first step in improving your financial acumen is to acknowledge its importance. Eventually, a lack of financial acumen will catch up with you. Imagine if I hadn't taken action to close my financial knowledge gaps while in my client director role at UCMS. At some point, the lagging financial performance of the contact centre, and my inability to adequately understand and interpret financial reporting and statements and then make remedial decisions, would have been noticed. If you are avoiding the numbers and still telling yourself that you're not good with numbers or that you prefer people over numbers, then now is the time to change that mindset. Otherwise, it will limit your career advancement.

The second step is understanding that financial acumen, like any other skill, can be learned and mastered with disciplined practice.

The third step is to evaluate where you are now. Ask yourself these questions:

- Do I understand and can I interpret financial statements, particularly the profit and loss, balance sheet and cash flow statements?
- Do I consistently apply financial concepts to support my judgment and business decision-making?
- Do I consistently make decisions in the context of the organisation's financial health?
- Do I consistently incorporate organisational financial information into my team's work?
- Do I proactively develop cost management strategies?
- Can I evaluate alternative financial scenarios before making a financial decision?
- Am I communicating in the language of the finance department to work more effectively and efficiently?
- Do I proactively facilitate the development of other people's financial acumen?

After you've answered these questions, then ask yourself:

- What are my financial acumen strengths, and am I effectively demonstrating them?

- What are my financial acumen weaknesses, and what will I do about them?

- How would my boss, or my boss's boss, respond to these questions about my financial acumen? (It is not enough to have financial acumen; you must be *known* as having these skills.)

Once you know what you need to work on, take the time to develop a plan to address your skill gaps intentionally. Here are some ideas for how to do this, no matter your career stage:

- **Tap your network.** Find opportunities to meet with other leaders whose skills can help you close the gap. Schedule a meeting with your finance team or partner to review your department's financial reports. Ask your finance business partner or internal accountant to analyse the impact of your (or your boss's) decisions.

- **Be curious.** Ask your boss and/or mentor to explain the financial concepts behind their decisions or recommendations. But do not just front up to the CFO and ask to be mentored without preparing! Part of your preparation is to be very clear about the financial skills and competencies you need to develop. Ask for their help to identify a suitable mentor or development activity for a defined period to help close your skill gaps. This approach provides the CFO with the opportunity to either take you on as a mentee or, if they do not have the capacity or appetite, refer you to a suitable substitute in their network.

- **Read more of the right stuff!** Business and finance publications that are related to your organisation and industry are particularly useful. I've already pointed out the value of reading your organisation's annual report (if your organisation is publicly listed) and highlighting the sections you do not understand, then discussing these with your boss in coaching sessions and with your finance mentor in mentoring sessions. Or, you can do what

I did and organise a regular meeting with your finance business partner to step you through things you do not understand.

- **Invest in continued professional development (CPD).** Do not assume that your boss knows financial acumen is an area for development for you, particularly if you are like I was and faking it a bit! Ask what courses are available to you through the company. I have a client who holds financial acumen lunch-and-learn drop-in sessions. The CFO and their team host them, and from all reports they are a terrific way to gain practical knowledge and skills. You may wish to find a program or short course designed for non-financial managers to develop financial skills with peers in similar situations. 'Finance for Non-finance Managers' is a popular short course across many tertiary institutions, and don't forget LinkedIn Learning: there are a plethora of options under the Finance and Accounting section.

The finance happy ending

After working at UCMS for almost four years, I became Executive General Manager, overseeing the company's largest division. My boss was the CEO, Denice Pitt. During my time there, I gained much experience and knowledge and continuously developed my financial acumen. While I may not have the same financial expertise as my wife, a finance professional, I am highly competent in reading and interpreting financial statements. Regardless of my role, I can analyse financial data and make informed decisions about the organisation's financial health. I am also recognised as a savvy businesswoman who took seriously the advice of my CEO about the importance of having – and being known for having – business, strategic and financial acumen.

You can do this too. Take this aspect of your development seriously. As Susan Colantuono says, 'It's never too early to develop your financial acumen, but at some point, it will probably be too late'.

Go deeper

Improving your business and financial acumen – understanding how a business operates, makes money and grows – is essential for making informed decisions and driving organisational success. Here is an activity to help you enhance your BQ and understand and improve your research skills, analytical thinking and ability to distil complex information into actionable insights:

1. Choose a publicly traded company you're interested in or one from an unfamiliar industry.

2. Research the company. Start by reading its profile on its official website. Understand its products, services and target audience. Read its annual report (usually available on its website under 'Investor relations'), focusing on the Chair/CEO's letter, the management discussion and key financial statements.

3. Analyse its financial statements. Look for its income statement, balance sheet and cash flow statement. Understand its revenue drivers (what's making it money), costs (where it's spending) and profits (how much it keeps). Note any significant year-on-year changes; these could point to market changes, company strategies or other external factors.

4. Analyse the market dynamics. Use resources like Google News or business news websites to understand recent events or trends affecting the company. Identify the company's main competitors and see if you can figure out what differentiates your chosen company from them. Download analysis reports and results presentations, often on the 'Investors Page' on the organisation's website, and use these to understand more about the organisation.

5. Summarise what you've learned. What does the company do well? Where are its challenges? What external factors affect its business? How does it compare to its competitors?

6. This step is optional but can be highly beneficial: share your insights with a friend, mentor or colleague. They might provide feedback or a different perspective that can deepen your understanding.

7. Think about how the insights you've gained might apply to your own work or business context. Are there lessons or strategies you can adopt?

8. Choose another company or industry and repeat the process. The more you practise, the more you'll refine your commercial acumen.

Go even deeper by getting your team involved. Instead of having boring team meetings, assign this activity to groups of people in your team, then ask them to report back on their insights at the next team meeting.

Take the Lead to Soar financial acumen self-assessment:

michelleredfern.com/thank-you-for-purchasing-my-book

Chapter 4

Lead Yourself

Leading yourself well is heavily influenced by the principles of emotional intelligence (EQ). In this chapter, I'll explore the importance of developing and mastering these EQ skills, because before you can effectively lead others, you must be able to lead and manage yourself. That means paying attention to your thoughts and feelings, and gaining actionable insights from your reflections to stay motivated and focused on what's important.

I am a strong and vocal advocate for reflective practice because I know from experience that regular reflective practice enables emotionally intelligent and high-performing leadership. The women who are the most coachable, and therefore most likely to accomplish great things, take time to stop, breathe and reflect on what has got them here, what still serves them and what no longer serves them.

The power of the emotionally intelligent leader

When I first started mentoring, coaching and developing women, I found three problems or opportunities women typically wanted help with.

Woman #1 is ambitious and driven. She wants to ascend to leadership and wants to know how to make that happen. She seeks me out to learn from my career journey and understand the skills she needs to develop to be considered ready for leadership.

Woman #2 has landed, or is about to land, her first prominent leader-of-leaders role. She's ascended to senior middle management and feels proud but a bit nervous, and in some cases she's worried that she's not as good as people think she is. She seeks me out to learn from my career journey, gain more confidence in herself and get advice about what to look out for so she can be successful.

Woman #3 is about to experience a significant life change, or has just done so. The change could be a milestone birthday, a change of employer, a retrenchment or redundancy, a kid leaving home, a divorce or recovery from an illness. She's usually been in the workforce for 20-plus years and has led a hectic life. She has been diligent and loyal to her employer and those around her, and has typically put everyone else first and herself last, but this life change has made her sit up and take notice of the way she feels about a bunch of things. She asks herself what she wants and does not want to do with the next chapter of her life. She seeks me out to learn from my career journey and to find clarity (and peace) about who the fuck she is and what the fuck she does now!

I have been all three types of woman. I wrote this chapter on EQ so you can avoid becoming Woman #3 and having a major WTF moment that derails your life, career and leadership aspirations.

My Woman #3 WTF moment

Around the time I turned 40 (first hint), I started to sleep very badly. I struggled to get to sleep, and when I eventually fell asleep, I tossed and turned and woke up frequently. This went on for weeks, until finally I told my (now) wife, Rhonda, 'That's it; I am going to the doctor to get some sleeping tablets'. She just nodded and said that she'd come along for moral support. So, off we trotted to our usual

GP, Dr Elise. Elise patiently listened to me complain about my poor sleep and request sleeping tablets. When I stopped talking, I expected a prescription to be written and handed over. Instead, Elise said, 'Tell me five things that make you happy'.

I spluttered, 'What?' So, she repeated the question: 'Tell me five things that make you happy'.

I was dumbfounded and infuriated, so I stared at her and then looked to Rhonda for support. She just shrugged. GAH! Elise then told me that I should go away, write down five things that made me happy and come back in a week to discuss them. I gracelessly acquiesced, grumbled something about unhelpful doctors and left, determined to write down five bloody happy things and return in two days!

Of course, I couldn't come up with five things to write down that made me happy. I struggled to think of two. I cried and returned to see Elise with my tail firmly between my legs. Elise did not prescribe me sleeping pills, but she did refer me to a counsellor to figure out what might be going on that was disrupting my sleep so badly. So, I went to see Chris, my counsellor, who in my first session made me realise that I'd experienced some significant changes in my life recently, such as:

- getting divorced from my children's father
- starting a new relationship with my same-sex partner
- coming out as gay to my family and friends
- moving house
- turning 40
- leaving the employer I had been with for 15 years
- starting a new, seriously senior job where they thought I was cleverer than I was (yes, that was my internal narrative).

Er, hello? These are major life events. But I had been so busy for so long that I had forgotten, or never learned, the importance of reflecting on my life. Who was I? What did I stand for? What made me tick? What made me happy? What should I do more of and less of to live well?

My inability to sleep was caused by my brain and body sending me very clear signals that I needed to stop being so damned busy and start caring for myself. This mindlessly busy life I was living was not enabling me to stop, breathe and reflect on how to be the best version of myself. I was not attuned to my emotions, and this no longer served me, my family or the people who depended on me to be a good leader.

EQ leadership lessons

In a 2012 *Harvard Business Review* article, Anthony K Tjan wrote:

> 'There is one quality that trumps all, evident in virtually every great entrepreneur, manager, and leader. That quality is self-awareness. The best thing leaders can do to improve their effectiveness is to become more aware of what motivates them and their decision-making.'

I was not adequately self-aware of my strengths and skills and how I brought them to life and leadership. I had not gained the skills to be emotionally resilient. If I didn't know myself well enough, how could I be the best version of myself, particularly regarding leadership, and have a soaring career? Over time, being constantly on the move and busy (that word!) meant that I had lost touch with who I was, what I stood for, how I wanted to do life and leadership and, of course, what made me happy.

Yikes. Work to do. However, I committed to doing the work, because I never again wanted to be in a position where my health, and my ability to do my job well and provide for my family, were compromised.

From that point on, I made the following commitments:

- **To continually focus on self-efficacy.** This means stopping my unhelpful behaviours and starting new, helpful ones. It also means constantly being on the lookout for new helpful behaviours to learn, such as mindfulness and breath work.

- **To adopt a growth mindset.** According to Professor Carol Dweck, having a growth mindset means that I understand I am not born with innate skills and can learn new skills through disciplined, intentional practice. I can use my grit and determination to master new skills, even if I fail the first time around. If at first you don't succeed, then try and try again.

- **To engage in reflective practice.** This means regularly taking the time to stop, breathe and reflect. Where am I now? What has got me here? What still serves me? What no longer serves me? What is it time for now? Reflective practice is not navel-gazing; it's taking the time to deliberately sift through life experiences to glean meaningful, actionable insights about events and behaviours.

- **To practise honest self-compassion.** Most of the time, I do my best. Irrespective of the outcome, I needed to be kinder and more compassionate to myself, because that, in turn, will help me to be more compassionate to others. Dr Kristin Neff, who has informed much of my self-compassion practice, says: 'With self-compassion, we give ourselves the same kindness and care we'd give to a good friend'.

- **To develop deep EQ competence.** According to Dr Daniel Goleman, EQ measures a person's ability to understand their emotions and those of others. People with well-developed EQ skills use these skills to guide their thinking and behaviour proactively. EQ relates to social and emotional competencies, and Goleman defines 12 competencies across four domains (see table 4.1, overleaf). 'To excel,' he says, 'leaders need to develop a balance of strengths across the suite of [EQ] competencies. When they do that, excellent business results follow'.

- **To understand my leadership style preferences.** This includes identifying styles that might be overused and are holding me back from being effective. I'll discuss the six leadership styles in more detail in the next chapter.

- **To write down what makes me happy and keep updating the list.** I have a section in my iPhone's notes app called 'My Happy ♥ List' and it has 56 entries. I use my happy list when I'm in a bit of a funk and need to disrupt myself and manage my emotional equilibrium more proactively.

- **To embrace the power of vulnerability.** I discuss vulnerability further in the next section.

Table 4.1: The 12 EQ competencies

Self-awareness	1. Emotional self-awareness
Self-management	2. Emotional self-control 3. Adaptability 4. Achievement orientation 5. Positive outlook
Social awareness	6. Empathy 7. Organisational awareness
Relationship management	8. Influence 9. Coaching and mentorship 10. Conflict management 11. Teamwork 12. Inspirational leadership

In summary, leaders must understand themselves so they don't become Woman #3, who doesn't know who the fuck she is and what the fuck she wants from life and leadership.

Vulnerability is a leadership game changer

The Oxford Dictionary defines vulnerability as 'being exposed to the possibility of being attacked or harmed, either physically or emotionally.'

Brené Brown describes vulnerability as 'uncertainty, risk, and emotional exposure'.

When I discovered that vulnerability is a leadership game changer, I decided to develop my own definition of vulnerability: 'Choosing to shed my armour, unlock my mistrust and strive to be courageous, loving and wholehearted in everything I do'.

I deliberately chose vulnerability after living and leading invulnerably for a long time. I was ambitious and driven from the outset of my career. I took great pride in being described as:

- tough
- uncompromising
- someone who gets shit done
- formidable
- a force to be reckoned with
- the fixer
- someone who is low maintenance and doesn't need help.

I had deliberately constructed and cultivated this persona over time. Many factors led to this – that might be a whole other book! – but, in essence, I was guided by what turned out to be a limiting belief that I needed to hold my own in business by:

- working harder
- partying harder
- shouting louder
- swearing harder (I still swear more than the average human!)
- being tougher
- being invulnerable.

I wore this behaviour like a suit of armour. Because when I was tough, formidable, uncompromising and a force to be reckoned with, no one messed with me, right? (Wrong.) And no one hurt me, right? (Wrong.)

Don't get me wrong, I don't think I was entirely an ogre. I was (and am) a lot of fun. But, given my private mantra was, 'Don't fuck with me or mine', I think there was an opportunity to examine how I was living my life!

Very few people saw me warts and all. They saw what I allowed them to see. It was exhausting having an internal me and an external me, particularly as I had committed to having well-developed EQ skills. I was self-aware enough to know what I was doing. However, I had pushed all reasonable thoughts about showing my true self to one side. I would deal with it. One day.

So, what happened? Did I have a grand epiphany, write an action plan and change? I did not. I saw a series of signals that I ignored and filed away for 'one day'.

I noticed one signal when talking to someone I'd been working with who had known me for a long time. We'd worked together in several different environments. I considered this person to know me very well. That person said to me, 'I'm glad you're here. We need someone to shake this place up who doesn't care too much about what people think, isn't emotional and can get shit done. You've got a hard heart and won't get sucked in.' That was the first signal. I was aghast... but I'm ashamed to say that part of me felt some satisfaction in being described that way.

Another signal appeared when, in continuing my commitment to lifelong learning, I started an MBA. One of my leadership units required self-analysis, reflection and planning to increase my effectiveness. I gained more valuable knowledge about myself. I had a couple of light-bulb moments. I constructed an action plan and I filed it for 'one day'.

Another cropped up when I was in the final stages of an interview for a role and the hiring exec had a chat with me about my reference checks – you know, the ones that happen without you knowing it? He had spoken to several people who had worked with me (they were all men, mind, but that is another conversation), and these guys said I was tough, did not tolerate fools gladly, got shit done and could be a bit of a hard case, but I was completely passionate and committed to my team, my work and my causes.

I wasn't surprised by this feedback, but it did worry me this time. I had achieved great success as an executive but felt stuck and unfulfilled. I realised that my habit of blaming others for difficult situations at work was holding me back from obtaining the role I wanted. I knew I needed to take responsibility for my actions and make changes. What had brought me success in the past was no longer sufficient.

But then I got a surprise. The hiring manager said, 'I see through you, Michelle. It's all a front. Because of circumstances, you've had to be tough and play hard, and now you're stuck with this persona you've created for yourself, aren't you? I know you're all that, but you're much more.'

Then he hired me, which was a game-changing moment.

I utilised that signal and the others filed away for 'one day' to alter my approach. I made a commitment to myself that I would use this new role as an opportunity to lose the persona, ditch the suit of armour and lead with truthfulness, transparency and vulnerability.

What had led me here was no longer enough. My behaviours were outdated and did not serve me or those who relied on me as a leader. Thus began my reinvention. Thus began the anxiety, because I was now about to create an environment of continuous emotional exposure.

Looking at it from a results-oriented perspective (as I still prioritise getting things done!), here are the benefits that came from leading with vulnerability:

- I achieved employee engagement scores of 88% in my first year and 92% in my second, significantly above the industry and organisational average. The reasons to strive for teams of highly engaged people are well documented, and I had developed a highly engaged, high-performing, highly productive and loyal team – the sort of team that people asked to come and work in. Yep, that felt good.

- I was regularly asked to be involved in deeply satisfying work. I began working on projects and initiatives inside and outside of work that were aligned with my purpose and leadership philosophy.
- I (eventually) quit my corporate job with the confidence to follow my bliss.
- Most importantly, I'm healthy and happy!

Vulnerability leadership lessons

Take a moment to stop, breathe and reflect on your current lifestyle. What choices have led you to this point? Which habits are still beneficial to you? Which are no longer helpful? To become a better leader, what actions should you prioritise, and what should you avoid?

Remember, life is not a practice run. Embrace your vulnerabilities and commit to living and leading wholeheartedly. Here are some steps you can take to do this:

- Document and share your leadership philosophy. (I'll cover this in more detail in later chapters.)
- Do not be afraid to ask for help.
- Delegate more. (Research by Susan Colantuono shows that this is a major development area for women.)
- Invoke boundaries and learn to say no.
- Put your hand up to do interesting new things, even scary ones!
- Admit that you do not know it all.
- Listen more.
- Try new things more.
- Embrace your flaws.
- Live a life of trying to give fewer fucks about what people think of you.

Go deeper

EQ measures a person's ability to understand their own emotions and those of others, and people use their EQ to guide their thinking and behaviour. When it comes to leadership, we must understand ourselves and our impact.

There are several things that you can do to improve your EQ:

- **Take an EQ assessment.** This can help you identify your strengths and weaknesses in terms of EQ.

- **Read books and articles on EQ.** A wealth of information is available on EQ, and reading about it can help you learn more about the different aspects of EQ.

- **Practise mindfulness.** Mindfulness is paying attention to the present moment without judgment. It can help you become more aware of your emotions and how they affect you.

- **Get feedback from others.** Ask your friends, family and colleagues for feedback on your EQ. This can help you identify areas where you can improve.

- **Seek professional help.** If you struggle to improve your EQ on your own, you may want to seek professional help from a therapist or coach who specialises in EQ.

Here is a reflective activity to help you think more deeply about your EQ:

- Which people and experiences in your early life had the greatest impact on you?

- What tools do you use to become self-aware? Who is your authentic self? When do you say to yourself, *This is the real me*?

- What are your most deeply held values? Where did they come from? Have your values changed significantly since your childhood? How do your values inform your actions?

- What motivates you extrinsically? What motivates you intrinsically? How do you balance extrinsic and intrinsic motivation in your life?

- What kind of support team do you have? How can your support team help you become a more authentic leader? How should you diversify your team to broaden your perspective?

- Is your life integrated? Can you be the same person in all aspects of your life – personal, work, family and community? If not, what is holding you back?

- What does being authentic mean in your life? Are you more effective as a leader when you behave authentically? Have you ever paid a price for your authenticity as a leader? Was it worth it?

- What steps can you take today, tomorrow and over the next year to develop your authentic leadership?

Do you want to stop, breathe and reflect? Then try the 'What's Your Story?' activity at michelleredfern.com/thank-you-for-purchasing-my-book.

Chapter 5

Lead Others and Organisations

I like to do things differently, to think outside the box and not be constrained by models, frameworks, rules and timelines. Consequently, questions such as, 'What do you want to be when you grow up?', 'Where do you see yourself in five years?', 'What are your long-term goals?' and 'Can we see your development plan?' used to unsettle me because I had no clear view of what I wanted to be.

While undertaking my MBA studies in 2014, I took a unit called Leading People and Organisations. My major assignment for that course was to produce an essay based on three questions about how to become a better leader:

1. What do I need to *know*?
2. What do I need to *do*?
3. What do I need to *be*?

Additionally, I was asked to consider what was holding me back from becoming a better leader of people and organisations.

I set about this task with the attitude that I can't 'do leadership' until I know what I need to know. And until I do what I need to do,

I can't be what I want to be, which is an outstanding and effective leader of people.

It should be abundantly clear by now that I want to share my learnings and expertise with more women because I want more women to be outstanding and effective leaders of people and organisations. For this to happen, women must identify what they need to know, do and be. This chapter builds on the principles and tools in chapter 3 and invites you to gain clarity about the frameworks, business models and level of cognitive and behavioural complexity you need to navigate your organisation and continually add value for the people you lead.

To be clear, I am using the terms 'leader' and 'manager' deliberately throughout the book, and they are not interchangeable. What is the difference between a manager and a leader, and does it matter? Yes, it does matter for any organisation wishing to achieve its goals, just as it should matter to a leader manager striving to be effective. John P Kotter tells us that management is about coping with complexity, planning, budgeting, organising and problem-solving, and leadership is about creating a vision, setting direction and coping with change. The world is an increasingly fast-paced and complex place. Therefore, the skills, competencies and traits associated with being an effective leader and manager must be known, understood and deployed by individuals and organisations for them to be successful.

In this chapter, I ask you to reflect on how your leadership behaviours affect others and your organisation.

Reflecting on leadership

My profession primarily involves communicating. According to my mother, I started talking at birth, and not much has changed since then! I focus my communications on leadership and how leaders must take action to create and sustain workplaces that work for every human, and especially women.

Without delving into politics, I always find it interesting and infor-mative to observe world leaders as they influence our planet. Whether you're a world leader or a leader in a workplace, you have at least one thing in common, which is that you'll likely be in an almost constant state of VUCA: volatility, uncertainty, complexity and ambiguity. Simply put, a lot is happening, and leaders must position themselves to anticipate the associated challenges and respond accordingly.

If VUCA is the hallmark of being a leader, how does it impact leaders intentionally leading others? Are leaders regularly stopping to consider what their leadership means to others? Are they reflecting on who is benefiting (or not) from their leadership style and approach?

Even though there are countless studies that have found women have superior EQ and leadership skills to men, I want women to think about their leadership impact more critically for two reasons. First, the research of my Lead to Soar co-founder and mentor Susan Colantuono reveals that if a woman takes her superior EQ and leadership as fact at any point in her career, she may think it's OK not to further develop these skills. As I've highlighted in previous chapters, focusing on self-efficacy, a growth mindset and CPD are the secret sauces associated with 'Type 1', make-it-happen people.

Second, the best, most coachable leaders systematically carve out time and space to reflect on their leadership performance, even when they don't like doing it! In a *Harvard Business Review* article, Jennifer Porter writes that leaders who don't make time for reflection are the toughest clients and, logically, are less likely to be effective leaders:

> 'Reflection gives the brain an opportunity to pause amidst the chaos, untangle and sort through observations and experi-ences, consider multiple possible interpretations, and create meaning. This meaning becomes learning, which can then inform future mindsets and actions.'

She suggests that perhaps one of the reasons these 'tough clients' don't undertake reflective practice is because they don't know how. So, let's get into some reflection!

Do you know what you cause?

Imagine being asked to introduce yourself to someone new with the following statement: 'Hi, my name is _____. I'm a leader, and I cause _____'. You may react similarly to how many others have when faced with this question: puzzled, confused and unsure of what to say.

If you've never done reflective practice, or tried and didn't find it effective, please find a method that works for you. I share some suggestions in the 'Go deeper' section at the end of this chapter.

In the meantime, I want you to stop, breathe and reflect on what you cause as a leader. What happens when you:

· walk into a room?
· walk out of a room?
· have a one-on-one conversation?
· facilitate or chair a meeting?
· attend a conference or expo?
· write an email?
· post on social media?
· walk around your workplace?

Do you cause people to:

· feel inspired and motivated?
· have clarity about the importance of their contribution to the organisation?
· seek your guidance, wisdom, knowledge, support and care?
· trust you?
· deliver great results aligned with the organisation's strategic and financial goals?

Or does something else happen? There is no time like the present for you to take ownership of understanding what your leadership causes.

When I consider what great leaders of people and organisations cause, I think of several things (see figure 5.1).

Figure 5.1: What great leaders of people and organisations cause

Emphasising the significance of EQ in leadership

In the previous chapter, I encouraged you to understand yourself deeply. In this chapter, I want to stress the importance of well-developed EQ skills to being a successful and authentic leader for your team and your organisation. This requires being intentional, thoughtful, attentive and transparent about how your leadership behaviour affects others. Or, as Dr Daniel Goleman states, 'IQ and technical skills are important, but emotional intelligence is the sine qua non (cause) of leadership'.

We know that technical skills and intellectual horsepower are essential and are gate-openers for senior and executive positions. However, the differentiator for those selected for and successful in executive roles will be EQ.

High-EQ leaders are crystal clear about how they show up, have clarity about what they cause and who they are in service of, and consistently deliver positive outcomes for people and organisations. Here are the outcomes that high-EQ leaders create:

· **They build trust and rapport with others.** They are more likely to be seen as approachable, which can help them build strong, strategic relationships with their team members and stakeholders.

- **They motivate and inspire their team members.** They can better understand what motivates them, both intrinsically and extrinsically, and create a sustainably motivating environment. They tap into their own innate enthusiasm and commitment to inspire and align others towards shared strategic goals.
- **They are adept at resolving conflict.** They are more likely to understand the underlying emotions in a conflict situation and look for ways to create shared understanding, if not consensus.
- **They handle stress and pressure.** They can better stay calm under pressure and make sound decisions even when stressed, which has a markedly positive impact on the people they lead. No one likes a panicky leader!
- **They make sound decisions.** They are attuned to the impact of their behaviour and decisions on the people around them and, consequently, will tend towards making decisions that are in the best interests of stakeholders.
- **They are adaptive leaders.** They are more likely to be able to embrace change and see it as an opportunity for growth, as well as understanding the need to draw from a range of leadership styles that suit the situation at hand.

The adaptive leader

Have you ever been asked what your leadership style is? As a panel judge for the Telstra Business Women's Awards, I always ask finalists that question. I learned a great many things from the inspiring businesswomen I interviewed, including the many different ways that women choose to lead. I also learned that if you ask six people what the best leadership style is, you will get six different answers – of course, because they are different people! After all, women are not one homogenous group. What I hear less often is people saying that a range of leadership styles should be used interchangeably depending on the situation at hand.

To be considered an effective leader of people and organisations, you must be capable of delivering results, which means utilising various managerial competencies and behaviours to optimise performance. Just as organisations do not adopt a one-size-fits-all method for getting work done, your effectiveness as a leader requires a parallel adoption of different strategies, competencies and styles.

This is the essence of leadership agility and adaptability. Andrea Clarke places adaptability at the top of her list of 'future fit' competencies in her book *Future Fit: How to stay relevant and competitive in the future of work*. Nothing is more certain than change, particularly in the organisational context. After all, for firms to maintain their competitive edge, they must continually reshape the way they do things. That means leaders must be adept at adapting, so we must add another 'Q' to the list: AQ (adaptability quotient/ intelligence) is an in-demand competency for leaders.

Effective, agile leaders are able to adapt their interpersonal leadership style to:

- bring out the best in team members and colleagues from diverse backgrounds
- facilitate psychologically safe environments to generate ideas and solutions
- manage situations with stakeholders who require nuanced communication
- challenge decision-making processes.

So, which leadership style works best? Goleman refers to the 'mystery' of effective leadership 'to spark the best performance' and ponders which precise leadership style provides the greatest results. The truth is that we must adapt our leadership style to suit the circumstances. The emotional intelligence framework gives some insights into what, when and how to employ these styles, and the impact of each (see table 5.1, overleaf).

Table 5.1: The six leadership styles

Leadership style	Operational approach	Key phrase
Coercive (Directive)	Enforces compliance swiftly	'Do what I say.'
Visionary (Authoritative)	Guides towards an overarching goal	'Join me on this journey.'
Harmonising (Affiliative)	Fosters a harmonious and inclusive environment	'People are our priority.'
Participative (Democratic)	Encourages collective decision-making	'What's your opinion?'
Exacting (Pacesetting)	Sets high standards for performance and leads by example	'Match my high standards.'
Empowering (Coaching)	Focuses on personal and professional growth of team members	'Have you considered this approach?'

Lead Others and Organisations

Core EQ skills	Optimal scenario for style	Impact on people and culture
Achievement drive, self-starting, self-regulation	Urgent crisis management, a performance turnaround strategy, remediating serious underperformance	Often negative (if sustained beyond the crisis)
Self-assurance, understanding others, initiating change	Assuming a new leadership role when a new direction or vision is essential	Strongly positive
Empathy, nurturing relationships, curiosity through effective dialogue	Mending team conflicts, boosting morale and providing reassurance during change	Generally positive
Team cooperation, leading inclusively and collaboratively, curious and respectful dialogue	When valuing team input or needing consensus, planning for change (building a coalition of the willing)	Generally positive
Diligence, ambition to excel, self-starting	When immediate results are needed from a competent and motivated team	Generally negative
Fostering others' growth, understanding others, self-insight	Assisting employee growth and developing future competencies	Positive

SOURCE: ADAPTED FROM HBR.ORG/2000/03/LEADERSHIP-THAT-GETS-RESULTS

Effective, agile and adaptive leaders do not rely on just one leadership style but instead use a variety of styles in different ways. You may have had a 'one-trick pony' for a manager, and in a business environment characterised by VUCA it's clear that a one-dimensional manager won't cut it. You must develop your understanding of different management frameworks so you can easily choose and apply the appropriate leadership style for the given situation.

The power of reflective practice

Do you feel like we've already discussed the power of reflective practice? You're right, and I will keep reinforcing that the most effective leaders invest in CPD and make time for reflection, asking themselves:

- Where am I now?
- What got me here?
- What still serves me?
- What do I need to do more of (to reach my full potential)?
- What do I need to do less of (to reach my full potential)?
- How do I get real about leadership?

Getting real as a high-EQ leader means taking the following actions:

- **Model emotional intelligence.** Be known as 'that high-EQ leader' by setting a good example. By demonstrating EQ through your behaviour, you will be aware of your own emotions, manage them effectively, and be able to understand and respond to the emotions of others.

- **Create an emotionally intelligent workplace.** Leaders can create an emotionally intelligent (which also means psychologically safe) workplace by fostering a culture of trust, respect and open communication. They also proactively provide opportunities for team members to learn about and develop their own EQ.

- **Empower team members.** Leaders give team members the responsibility and authority to make decisions. This can help them feel more confident and in control of their work – and let's face it, no one likes being micromanaged!

While technical skills and intelligence are important for senior and executive positions, being a high-EQ leader means having clarity about yourself, your actions and who you serve so you can consistently deliver positive outcomes for the people and organisations you lead.

Now, it's time for you to go deeper.

Go deeper

> 'Stand upright, speak thy thought, declare the truth thou
> hast, that all may share. Be bold. Proclaim it everywhere.
> They only live who dare.'
>
> – Voltaire

Reflecting on, writing down and discussing my leadership philosophy has been one of the most beneficial exercises I've ever undertaken. It has allowed me to deeply consider my life experiences, my leadership journey, and the individuals and situations that have influenced me. This process has played a pivotal role in my personal and professional development.

I want you to be aware of what you want to cause, who you are in service to and who you are called to become, and declare it! So, I encourage you to develop your leadership philosophy.

The concept of developing a leadership philosophy is not new. It is common practice in the United States Armed Forces for top-ranking officials to develop and declare their leadership philosophy. The process I followed to develop my leadership philosophy did not happen quickly. The initial part of the exercise took over a month. Committing to reflecting on my lifetime leadership journey, the events that formed me, the people who shaped me and the experiences that taught me was an incredibly personal exercise that made me feel very vulnerable. But it was worth it, as I developed the words and phrases that underpinned how I worked, and what people could depend on me for, as a leader.

I have been updating, shaping, refining and declaring my leadership philosophy since I created it nearly a decade ago. My leadership philosophy is my north star; it's how I guide myself in living, working and leading. I hope to inspire you to develop your leadership philosophy and then share it.

My leadership philosophy (what I cause)

I want to make a difference no matter what I do, and I am often not satisfied with the status quo. I have little tolerance for cultures of blame or people who shirk their responsibilities and duty. I always work with a positive, growth mindset and do everything I can to create an environment in which people know what they need to contribute and can succeed by ensuring they have a clear purpose, vision and roadmap. I lead from the front but not too far in front. What that means to me and the people I lead is that I promise to create a vision, take them on a journey and then get out of the way to allow them to shine but be there when they need me. And I always keep my promises.

I loathe labels and boxes. I am called to become a leader who challenges the world to rid itself of unnecessary boxes, labels and other limiting beliefs and behaviours. I don't like being assigned to a one-dimensional category as no single category could possibly describe the complex, flawed, passionate, energetic, positive human I am, and I promise not to do that to anyone else. And I always keep my promises.

I am called to become a champion of, and a positive role model for, women. I am called to advance women's rights worldwide. I promise to continue to be courageous, give my whole self, be purposeful and always endeavour to understand what I cause.

I continually seek to better understand the story of my life and glean meaning from my experiences. I try my best to embrace vulnerability, hold myself to account, be guided daily by this leadership philosophy and always understand what I cause.

Develop your leadership philosophy

A leadership philosophy defines how we see ourselves as leaders. This philosophy guides our actions, our behaviours and our thoughts. External and internal forces influence our philosophy. We can change who we are as leaders by simply changing our leadership philosophy; leadership philosophies can change as we grow to understand ourselves within the context of leading.

To start developing your leadership philosophy, consider these questions:

· Think for a moment about the best boss you've ever had. What was it that made working with them so rewarding?

· Now, think about the worst boss you've ever had. What was it that made working with them so damned hard?

· Now, consider your leadership style from the perspective of your colleagues. What makes it easy or hard to work with you?

What do your answers mean for your leadership style and approach? What actionable insights have you gained about what you cause?

Creating or finding your leadership philosophy means exploring and reflecting on your values and beliefs about leadership:

· **Values** are qualities or characteristics that you consider important. You would rather leave an organisation or step down as a leader than violate your values. Your values guide your intentions and influence how you lead. When your values are clear, and you're conscious of them, you create a solid foundation for leading – and, importantly, people see you leading in alignment with your declared values.

- **Beliefs** are ideas we hold to be true and which shape our realities. For example, if a leader believes that the only individuals in an organisation who can make decisions are the management staff, that belief will influence how the leader treats others. Beliefs can also be unconscious; they are a habitual way of thinking and acting. So, if your core belief system is left uninterrupted or unexamined, then it will unconsciously dictate your thoughts, feelings and leadership behaviours. When I am asked to discuss unconscious bias with workplace leaders, I talk instead about our belief systems and how they may inadvertently get in the way of us being the best leaders we can be.

The activity 'How to Develop Your Leadership Philosophy' at michelleredfern.com/thank-you-for-purchasing-my-book will help you create, find or define your leadership philosophy.

Chapter 6

Confidence Conundrum

Once upon a time, I was outwardly confident. Now, I am both outwardly *and* inwardly confident; in other words, I have banished the little voice in my head that used to tell me I wasn't enough. That little voice, often called 'imposter syndrome' by others, plagued me for many years.

Before I tell you about how I banished the loud negative voice in my head, I want to call bullshit on something: I am heartily sick of imposter syndrome being discussed in the context of women. Imposter syndrome is a symptom of a system that still places almost insurmountable barriers in front of women who want to succeed. To hark back to earlier in the book, it is the system that needs fixing, *not* women!

As career coach Kashia Dunner puts it:

'Imposter syndrome is a phrase that I'm not even entertaining anymore because it feels like career gaslighting. Women and other underrepresented groups aren't suffering from imposter syndrome; they're suffering in a system that wasn't designed with their success in mind.'

Systemic bias often leads to women being labelled less ambitious, even when it's false. Stefanie O'Connell Rodriguez says there is no ambition gap, but there is an ambition penalty. In dozens of conversations with women, she learned that while women have been told to speak up and take ownership of their career advancement, they are punished for doing so. In my thousands of conversations with women they tell me that they are told they are too money-motivated, unlikeable and bossy. They are told to stay in their lane, given less credit for their work and accused of not acting as they are supposed to. No wonder women stop asking.

Compounding this issue is the fact that decision-makers place far too much emphasis on people who present as confident and charismatic rather than competent and credible. In his book *Why Do So Many Incompetent Men Become Leaders? (And How to Fix It)*, Tomas Chamorro-Premuzic says managers cannot discern between confidence and competence. Because of this, society is tricked into believing that men are more confident than women, when in reality 'manifestations of hubris' occur more frequently in men. I often ask people in my gender dynamics workshops if they'd rather have a confident or competent brain surgeon.

In 2000, David Dunning and Justin Kruger published a paper titled 'Unskilled and unaware of it: how difficulties in recognising one's own incompetence lead to inflated self-assessments'. The study found that people who are incompetent in a particular domain lack the skill to recognise their lack of skill, and so they grossly overestimate their own competence.

Here is the thing: we *all* know someone who has been elevated to a position of responsibility beyond their range of competency. I argue (with confidence, based on the research of the respected folks I've mentioned) that it is more likely than not that someone was a bloke. He will have given himself top-notch self-assessment ratings, saddled up his ego and rode boldly where many men have gone before. (Donald Trump, anyone?)

So, coming back to the confidence conundrum and imposter syndrome, if we must use the term 'imposter syndrome' then let's get real. Fear of failure, feeling like you don't deserve to be where you are, feeling like you don't belong and feeling unworthy are not exclusive to women.

However, I acknowledge that the response to these fears may differ among genders, particularly in environments where rigid gender stereotypes prevail. For example, suppose a man experiencing self-doubt, lacking confidence or fearing failure is in a tough, blokey workplace. In that case, he will likely mask his feelings, suppress them and pretend that he is OK rather than making himself vulnerable to criticism and ridicule. Research tells us that when women feel vulnerable, scared or anxious, they are more likely to verbalise these feelings and seek support. This is perhaps one reason women are lumbered with the 'imposter syndrome' label more often than our male counterparts: we talk about it more!

Leaders of all genders must be very wary of conversations about imposter syndrome in the workplace and think more critically about this matter. Is it a lack of confidence or imposter syndrome that you're seeing, or is it a woman trying to navigate the murky waters of gender bias and discrimination? Is this conversation gendered – that is, are we only discussing a lack of confidence in women – or are we assessing people of all genders the same way? Let's take our leadership responsibility seriously and allow everyone to be more self-assured by creating and sustaining inclusive environments where folks can discuss how they think and feel in a safe space.

OK, rant over.

My confidence conundrum

I left high school in the mid-1980s when I was 15. That wasn't a particularly radical thing to do, especially in a regional town in the Mid West region of Western Australia. My parents were devastated as they had worked hard to provide better opportunities for their three girls than they'd had, which included them having to finish school at 14 to contribute financially to their families.

Nonetheless, I was determined to leave because I had been offered a full-time job, and the prospect of being financially independent was enticing. My best negotiation skills came to the fore and, finally, Mum and Dad signed the form for me to leave at the end of Year 10.

Fast-forward 25 years to the turn of the 2010s. A lot of water had flowed under my bridge of life by that stage, including, as you've already read, catapulting myself into the private sector after a 15-year career at Telstra. I had a brilliant job and a terrific new executive role, I was earning great money and I felt supremely confident about my place in the world.

On the outside.

On the inside, my self-talk would go something like this:

'How did a high-school dropout get to do this job?'

'One day, someone is going to figure out that not only did you not go to university, but you didn't even finish high school.'

'You're lucky you've had good managers who have looked after you.'

'You're not as good as everyone thinks you are.'

I thought I wasn't smart enough, I didn't belong and I had only accomplished what I had accomplished through some accident or luck. I was fortunate that my fundamental lack of self-belief and inner dialogue did not derail me or my career. I have a determined 'soldier on' mindset, but my noisy inner critic took up energy that could have been better used elsewhere.

I was fortunate to participate in some outstanding professional development activities. Over a decade, I gained business management skills, people management skills and technical skills associated with my different roles, as well as various coaching accreditations. I undertook short courses and was a voracious reader of anything about business.

I also performed to a high standard in my workplaces. I received some awards, was a member of two high-potential programs at Telstra and UCMS, and became an executive running a $100 million division for a global business process outsourcing (BPO) firm that I joined in 2010 after a couple of years working in the third-party logisitics (3PL) industry.

But still, my inner critic persisted.

Back to school

After a conversation with a colleague who had a similar education and career background as me, and in consultation with Rhonda, I decided to embark upon an Executive MBA. It would finally get this monkey off my back and provide me with a tertiary qualification so I could never get caught out. This was a challenging undertaking, both financially and logistically. Aside from the extensive travel requirements of the executive role I was holding, there was the eye-watering cost of the MBA, which, combined with a healthy mortgage and financial responsibilities for my offspring, meant some serious belt-tightening would need to occur in our family.

All so I could kick my imposter syndrome to the kerb once and for all. Good grief.

Anyway, off I went to RMIT University for a four-day intensive course called Business in the Global Context. This was followed by a semester of Accounting for Business Decisions.

I vividly remember being in my first Accounting lecture. It was a smallish cohort of 20 people, mostly men. The lecturer, Sam, asked everyone to introduce themselves. I had a significant 'oh shit' moment as I heard the roles of my classmates: CEOs, CFOs and other important-sounding titles. I felt out of place, like I didn't belong and was not worthy enough to be in this class. I finally introduced myself, and we went on with the class.

Then something amazing happened: Sam asked a question about a particular accounting principle, and I knew the answer!

So, I answered. Correctly. Then there was another question, and again I knew the answer (but I shut up this time to let someone else have a go). Then we moved on to another principle, and I confidently discussed it with the people I was in a small group discussion with.

I walked out of that lecture – actually, I think I floated – feeling more inwardly confident about my abilities than I ever had before.

I threw myself into my MBA with gusto. To say that I loved the experience would be an understatement. Yes, I learned some new things and gained some new skills, but my biggest discovery was that I was smarter than I had ever given myself credit for. That discovery came about because my studies fostered deep reflection and learning about my leadership style, the skills I already had and the skill gaps I needed to close to meet my career goals. I realised I was intelligent, innovative and entrepreneurial, and wouldn't be found out!

I became less afraid and more courageous. And you know what else? The more I discovered my innate strengths, traits and characteristics, the less I cared about bending myself out of shape to meet the unrealistic expectations that imposter syndrome creates.

The added bonus of studying is that it helped me become a more rounded, complete and interesting person. Studying made me happy. It gave me a focus outside of my work. It created the need for discipline to balance my work hours with the hours I allocated to study and leisure. I became a better role model, because women in my workplace benefited from seeing someone like me add an MBA study load to my life, and prioritise and manage it well.

Does every woman need to undertake further education to banish imposter syndrome? Of course not. But every woman needs to stop, breathe and reflect on what is causing her lack of confidence and then take action to address that.

My wise friend and mentor Susan Colantuono says, 'In business, confidence rests on a foundation of leadership competencies'. You need to have a strong base of leadership competencies to avoid faking it. We already have enough fakers in the business world, so let's crack on and assess which skills you need to brush up on, why, when and how.

How to confidently navigate your brilliant, soaring career

'Fake it 'til you make it' is poor career advice and highly gendered. As I've already discussed, men benefit from the positive assumption that they are competent, so they will more often put themselves forward for a role even if they are underqualified.

In 2018, I was engaged by one of Australia's largest insurance firms, Insurance Australia Group (IAG), to design and deliver a women's leadership program. The program is called 'Game Changers' and aims to help women develop and demonstrate critical business skills, and to help IAG close their leadership gender gap. The content of the program is centred on business, strategic and financial acumen skills, and I am especially proud of it. In 2019, Suzanne Storrie, who was Executive General Manager of Finance and Operations at IAG at the time and is now a Non-Executive Director, was the program's executive sponsor. In one session, she recounted to the group that she was advertising for a senior role and was seeing first-hand the phenomenon that men apply for a role when they have just a few required skills, whereas women won't apply unless they have *all* the skills. She said she had received applications from men who were barely qualified for the role, yet she knew women who were suitable candidates but hadn't applied.

What's the moral of this story for women? Please have a go! If you do not ask, the answer will always be 'no'. Leaders and talent-sourcers, please look harder for talented women. They are out there but are navigating decades of bias and discrimination, which saps their confidence to apply for roles.

A brilliant, soaring career depends on CPD – in other words, building your levels of knowledge and experience. CPD is the ongoing process of developing professional skills and knowledge through interactive, participation-based or independent learning. When I was completing my MBA, I read in a management journal that career-building is 'a journey to mastery that is never complete'. What a great way to describe my love of learning and how I have created a brilliant, soaring career.

CPD is important because one-and-done PD doesn't cut it. One course, one conference, one book or one article will never enable a woman to develop her professional capabilities to their fullest potential. Proactively and continually investing time and effort in formal, informal and self-guided learning is essential for career success.

For those of you in the medical, legal or finance professions, or who are members of a professional body, you will be aware that CPD requirements are laid out for you by your professional body. In my case, as a professional non-executive director, I must evidence my CPD hours and activity to maintain membership and accreditation to my industry association, the Australian Institute of Company Directors (AICD).

Leadership is a profession. Leadership is my vocation. Therefore, I invest in CPD of my leadership skills and knowledge so that I can fulfil not only the duties of a leader but also enjoy my role as a leader, mentor, guide and developer of more leaders.

Employers also increasingly expect their staff to undertake CPD and may even measure them on it. Evidencing your time, effort and commitment to honing your leadership skills is a terrific way to demonstrate to your boss and other strategic stakeholders your commitment to advancing the business. As someone who has hired hundreds of people and now find myself influencing the hiring of CEOs and executives, I look for evidence of the candidate being a self-starter, particularly when it comes to the continuous development of skills and knowledge.

Regardless of whether CPD is mandatory or discretionary, the most satisfying results are achieved by professionals who drive their own CPD. Women with soaring careers do not wait until there is an urgent need to satisfy professional registration requirements or until their manager points out areas for improvement.

Women with soaring careers do six things:

1. They reflect on their strengths and use them sensibly. Strengths can be overused or overly relied upon. For example, I used to rely too much on my EQ skills, which meant I didn't focus enough on my gaps – particularly my financial acumen.

2. They identify their skills and knowledge gaps, and then develop strategies to mitigate and manage those gaps.

3. They listen to and *act* on *relevant* career advice or feedback from their manager and sponsors.

4. They remain alert to CPD opportunities and assess their relevance to their career plan or leadership development needs. Even if you're like me and don't have absolute clarity on your next big move, there will be themes you've identified by reading this book that will inform you about where to focus your CPD.

5. They devote time (and effort) to career planning and CPD planning.

6. They regularly discuss with their manager aligning their CPD interests and the organisation's needs. (This is very helpful if you want your organisation to invest in your CPD!)

Reflect on your commitment to CPD

It is essential to frequently assess and reflect upon your commitment to CPD as a leader. This includes tallying the hours you've dedicated to CPD and evaluating the nature and quality of those experiences, whether they were courses, reading materials, conferences, coaching, mentoring, online education or networking.

Discussing the CPD you've undertaken with your manager in your annual performance review, and the CPD you plan for next year, is essential. Your manager needs to know about your commitment to your CPD – they are not mind-readers! – and this helps shape their perception of you. Also, your CPD can be a component of a non-cash compensation package. If your boss knows your plans, there may be room in the budget to fund some of your activities!

I was able to negotiate having my AICD accreditation being paid for by my employer. The context was that I had taken on a new role, an internal promotion, but I was already at the high end of the salary band, and the timing of my appointment was outside of the normal remuneration review cycle. You know what is coming, don't you? Both these factors meant I did not receive a salary bump to recognise the promotion. I was a bit grumpy about it, until I realised that rather than pushing hard for something that was not going to happen at that time, I could secure an alternative commitment from my manager. He agreed to fund my AICD accreditation (circa $9000, plus time to attend the course and study for the exam), and when the annual remuneration review cycle came around he guaranteed me a percentage increase in my base salary. It was a win-win: a win for me for my CPD and salary, and a win for the organisation because they got an engaged, enthused executive who was going to stick around and bring new skills to her role.

I have always found it helpful to block out the time I plan to devote to CPD and diversify my activities to ensure a comprehensive and well-rounded skill enhancement. For example, there is a specific podcast I listen to (*Take on Board* by Helga Svendsen) that contributes to my CPD as a non-executive director. I save up the episodes and listen to four at a time once a month. Yes, that time is in my diary so I can evidence it as part of my CPD for the AICD. I also plan time for reading the AICD *Company Director* magazine and other business magazines I subscribe to. When I worked in the corporate sector, I would block out time in my calendar every week for deep thinking or reading, because if I tried to fit self-directed CPD around all my other competing priorities then it just wouldn't happen. I also looked at what additional skills and qualifications I wanted to gain that aligned with my immediate career objectives.

There a wise adage, 'If it is to be, it is up to me'. This holds especially true for your CPD. Don't wait for someone else to send you to a training course or assign you a mentor. Take charge by investing in your leadership development. It is a lifelong journey, and it's important to regularly reflect and plan to stay on track so you can establish yourself as a self-motivated learner who consistently puts time and effort into formal, informal and self-directed education.

Go deeper

It's time to reflect on your commitment to CPD:

- How many hours of CPD have you invested in so far this year to develop your leadership skills and knowledge?
- What has your CPD consisted of? (Courses? Reading? Conferences? Coaching? Mentoring? Online learning? Networking?)
- How many hours of CPD will you invest in for the rest of the year to develop your leadership skills and knowledge?
- What activities will your CPD plan include?

The Lead to Soar Network is the perfect example of women committing to CPD. After women join Lead to Soar, they tell me that they achieve better results, better salaries, better bosses and better jobs due to the extraordinary support, coaching, mentoring and resources they have access to in the network. The best thing about Lead to Soar is that your organisation can join as a corporate member, or you can ask your organisation to fund your membership as it is legitimately continuing professional development for women. Check it out at leadtosoar.network.

Chapter 7

Be Your Own CEO

It's a small world! This is a very old saying that is often used when we realise, with surprise, how interconnected the people we know are. This is exemplified by the theory of the six degrees of separation. In the 1960s, social psychologist Stanley Milgram ran an experiment in which a few hundred people in Boston and Omaha in the USA had to get a letter to a target, a perfect stranger in Boston – but the only way they could do this was by posting the letter to someone in their network who they thought might be closer to the target person than them. When Milgram looked at the letters that reached the target, he found that the letters had changed hands only about six times.

In the 21st century, it's easy to imagine that six degrees of separation could be halved, given we live in a highly connected, 24/7 digital world of emails, social media and other digital connection points. In this context, my rapidly advancing career and lofty aspirations forced me to be much more considerate and purposeful about how I showed up in our interconnected world. I don't believe I had any one revelation about the importance of my personal brand, but I certainly had some signposts along the way that helped me to realise a few things:

- I am a committed leader of the organisation I work for, but that organisation is *not* my personal brand.
- I am responsible for curating and cultivating my leadership brand.
- My leadership brand is what makes me stand out.
- I am my own CEO.

Becoming CEO of my own personal brand

I recall that one of the first signposts for my decision to become my own CEO was the advent of LinkedIn. LinkedIn was founded in 2002, launched in 2003 and came onto my radar in 2006 when I was an executive at UCMS. I had started accelerating my executive career in this call centre outsourcing company. We had an executive who was charged with expanding our sales and marketing capability, and as part of that they introduced us to LinkedIn.

I took to LinkedIn like a duck to water. However, I had to confront some cold, hard, brutal truths when I set about creating my LinkedIn profile and starting to use the platform. I wasn't just Michelle Redfern, an executive at UCMS – I was so much more. But not enough people knew my 'so much more' story.

I realised that I needed to get serious about my brand (not that I would have used that language in 2008). Part of getting serious was to start following and learning from people who were good at this stuff!

When I was on the other side of a messy, awful divorce with no assets, I realised two things. First, nothing was worth more than the custody of my two beautiful children. Second, I was my best asset in providing for my family. I was talented and ambitious and could potentially attain leadership positions with great earning potential. If only more people in the business world knew that!

Did anyone who mattered in the business world know that I was a great asset? My previous bosses and my current bosses did. But did potential future bosses, organisations and other influential stakeholders know what a great asset I was to the organisation I worked for? Nope!

It was time to get serious about cultivating and curating my best product and asset: me! It was time for michelleredfern.com to be founded. Effective CEOs know their product, market and value proposition, and set the company's brand awareness and equity agenda. So, on that basis, I decided to get comfortable with the fact that I was (and still am) a brand and the CEO of that brand. I asked myself, *Is my personal brand being defined by me, or am I allowing my brand to be determined by others?*

Before I get into the 'what' and 'how' of personal branding, I want to share a cautionary tale about being branded by others.

The dangers of letting your brand be defined by others

In 2010, I was an executive for a BPO firm. My role as General Manager of BPO Operations in Australia included client relationship and contract management. We had major accounts with various Australian Government departments, and I was negotiating with a new department to secure the contract for a new contact centre. The negotiations with the client took place by email and teleconference. As the negotiations approached their end, it came time for me to visit the client in Canberra to hammer out the final few details and begin building relationships with the key people in the department.

Off I went to Canberra. I turned up at the office building where the meeting was to be held, signed in and made my way to the assigned room. There were a handful of people there. I asked them if they were my clients, as I did not know what my clients looked like. They reassured me that they were the people I was there to meet. Excellent. The meeting kicked off.

Later, as we chatted more socially, I asked if they wondered whether I was the right person when I entered the room. The most senior bureaucrat there laughed and said, 'Oh goodness no, we knew it was you Michelle because we googled you!' Haha, good one, I thought. But then I had another thought. What on earth is on Google about me?

I surreptitiously grabbed my iPhone and googled myself. Up came my LinkedIn profile and a couple of articles I had contributed to. *Hmm, that's OK*, I thought. Then, I clicked on 'Images', and my stomach lurched. The first image of me on Google was from my Facebook page and had been taken at my birthday party the year before. I was holding a champagne glass aloft, toasting the camera, poking my tongue out and generally looking like a party girl. I wanted my clients to consider me as a seriously commercially savvy, hard-nosed negotiator who wasn't to be trifled with, a worthy adversary across the negotiation table; this image did *not* enhance that perception. I had potentially lost control of my brand by posting a funny picture on social media.

At that point, I decided to be even more intentional and diligent about what I posted online, and I locked down my privacy settings on my personal social media profiles. That included not allowing myself to be tagged in photos on Facebook, Instagram or Twitter.

Fortunately, the image was relatively innocuous, and the clients were terrific people. But I learned my lesson: brand or be branded!

How to start developing your brand

Personal branding has a myriad of definitions. One is, 'Personal branding is a marketing strategy focused on your most important product: you'. Another is, 'Your personal brand is what people say about you when you aren't in the room'.

Michelangelo said, 'Every block of stone has a statue inside it, and it is the sculptor's task to discover it'. The same is true of your brand. You don't create your brand; you already have one, and it's your job to reveal it and make it shine.

My brand is my calling card. Once I understood how I wanted to be perceived, I could start being much more strategic about making my brand shine.

Your brand is all about, as Susan Colantuono says, 'using the greatness in you'. The greatness in you comprises your attributes, strengths, values, worldview and personal purpose.

Crafting a memorable and impactful statement requires careful planning and practice. Being your own CEO goes beyond buzzwords or a catchy title. Developing your brand is crucial if you want to make an impact. Like any effective CEO, understanding, nurturing and positioning your 'product' – which is you – is imperative. You already have a brand, whether consciously crafted or passively shaped by external factors, so be intentional and proactive about the narrative you want to portray.

Personal branding is not about ego or vanity. Rather, it an essential tool for you to recognise and amplify your unique strengths, attributes and value proposition. Regular reflection, leveraging tools to understand your strengths and consistently aligning your actions will result in establishing an authentic leadership brand that resonates with the audiences you seek to influence. As Michelangelo unveiled the beauty within the block of stone, you must reveal your brand's brilliance to the world. Always remember that you are the best advocate for your brand, so brand intentionally, consistently and brilliantly.

Mindset is the key to developing your brand. You cultivate your brand daily, even if you don't realise it. How you think, speak, communicate and write (including posting on social media) all add to the overall impression you create, which is your brand. The power to cultivate it, or not, rests with you.

The first step in the personal branding process is to figure out who you are and what you want from your career. I created a set of questions to help myself sculpt out the heart of my brand:

- What do people think about when they hear or see my name?
- Are there subjects that I want people to associate with my name?

- How do I want to be perceived in my chosen market? (Note that my chosen market was often my current employer.)
- What do I want to be known for?
- What do I stand for?

Another exercise I undertook was to select five words to describe myself from the list at kevan.org/johari, then ask trusted colleagues and friends to describe me in one word. I then compiled the responses in a Johari window (see figure 7.1): words mentioned both by me and a colleague or friend go in the 'Open self' box, words mentioned only by me go in the 'Hidden self' box and words mentioned only by colleagues or friends go in the 'Blind self' box (and the remaining words from the original list go in the 'Unknown self' box). The Johari window is not everyone's cup of tea, but I appreciate it because it provides a safe, anonymous way for you to discover potentially hidden strengths about yourself. This was powerful because when I selected five words to describe myself, there were some interesting deviations from my audience's responses. Used in conjunction with other diagnostic tools, the Johari window can be a powerful way to increase your self-awareness about the attributes and strengths that form your personal brand.

Figure 7.1: The Johari window

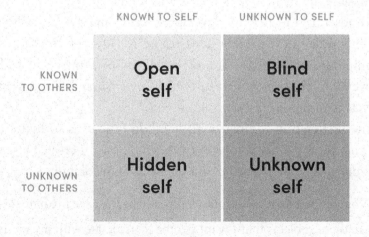

A tool I encourage people to use to get to the heart of who they are and what they are great at is the Gallup CliftonStrengths® assessment. I've used this tool to better understand myself and what I did best to create a congruent, aligned self-belief. I've also used it with teams I've led and clients I've coached.

Creating your brand statement

Once you have identified your brand, you can communicate it in various ways. First, it can serve as the foundation for your LinkedIn profile, CV and professional bio. Second, it can help you create an effective elevator pitch, which is crucial when introducing yourself in person.

Follow this five-step process to communicate your brand in our interconnected world:

1. Identify your goal. Is this brand statement going to help you get a new job, or more customers, or something else? Strategically tailoring your statement to your objectives and your chosen market will make it more effective.

2. Write out your personal brand statement in long form. Aim for a couple of paragraphs. Incorporate the work you've just done to identify your core attributes, values and strengths. (When you create your 'I am known for my' sentence at the end of this chapter, you can incorporate that, too.). Let people know what you bring, how you show up and what people can expect from you. Be brave and speak out about your aspirations and potential. Be descriptive; it is better to write too much and refine it over time than not write enough. Be real; people have very good BS detectors, so don't try to be someone you're not. And be memorable!

3. Use a tool like Grammarly or even ChatGPT to check that grammar is correct, you're being descriptive but concise and you're not overusing words.

4. Read your brand statement out loud. Tweak it as necessary.

5. Ask a trusted colleague or mentor to review it and provide feedback. Tweak again.

6. Use your brand statement as a base for your LinkedIn, CV and bio (remembering that your CV and bio should always be tailored to the audience and situation).

Here are two of my bios that I provide to clients when they need to introduce me to an audience; I hope you find them useful and they inspire you to create your own:

1. Michelle Redfern is an award-winning advisor and experienced facilitator known for her inspiration and boundless energy. As a leading advocate for women's advancement, she has been recognised as one of Australia's Top 100 Women of Influence, winning awards for her outstanding efforts. Her passion lies in creating workplaces that work for every human.

2. Michelle Redfern is a globally recognised gender diversity, equity and inclusion (DEI) strategist. She advises organisations in the business and sporting sectors on DEI strategy development and implementation, and works directly with women leaders to advance their careers.

CEO introduction

Have you ever wondered why it is called an elevator pitch? Ponder this: you've just bumped into a former boss in the airport lounge. After exchanging pleasantries, they ask you what you do now. You open your mouth and then pause. Where on earth do you start? You blather on with some lightweight pleasantries. Then, as you try to organise your thoughts, boarding commences for their plane and they are on their way. Opportunity lost. If only you'd had a short speech – about the duration of an elevator ride – ready to go.

If you'd been better prepared, you're sure you would have told them what's important to you and your organisation, and you would have strengthened your brand and your connection with your former boss. This is just one situation in which it helps to have a powerful, memorable elevator pitch or CEO introduction. This short, pre-prepared speech explains what you do and what your current priorities are. When people ask who you are or what you do, this is how you answer. Me?

This is one of my CEO introductions (I have a few, depending on my audience and the circumstances):

> 'My job is to close the global leadership gender gap, and
> I do that in two ways. Firstly, I help fix in workplaces that
> prevent women and their organisations from reaching their
> full potential; and secondly, I work with women to help them
> navigate a system that still has barriers to their advancement.'

You can develop your CEO introduction (elevator pitch) by identifying:

- the problems you solve
- the value you create
- the outcomes you deliver.

Your CEO introduction should be 30 seconds maximum – you want to leave people curious and interested to ask more. If you are holding a lit match between your forefinger and thumb, you should be finished introducing yourself by the time the match burns down.

Practise the way you introduce yourself, too. Listen to my *Lead to Soar* podcast episode 'How to Nail a Confident Introduction' for more tips.

I hate to be the bearer of bad news, but there is no substitute or shortcut for practice. So, find a trusted colleague or mentor and practise, practise, practise. This leadership skill will become increasingly important as your career advances.

Go deeper

I like this exercise I adapted, with permission, from *No Ceiling, No Walls* by Susan Colantuono. Draw up a page with two columns. In the first column, write down your core attributes and values, and describe why they are your values and how they shape how you show up as a leader. In the second column, write your strengths, which are skills that you have become accomplished in (see table 7.1).

Table 7.1: Your core attributes and values, and strengths

Core attributes and values	Strengths
e.g., sense of humour, inclusiveness, stamina and resilience, compassion *I use humour to build rapport and make people feel relaxed and safe with me, which means I am more likely to hear what I need to hear rather than what people think they want me to hear.*	e.g., strategic thinking, business planning, collaboration, relationship management, technical or industry skills *I am able to lift myself out of my day-to-day tasks to think about the future and what strategies my team will need to navigate the challenges and exploit the opportunities.*

Your superpowers are the sum of your attributes, values and strengths. They are what make you stand out and what you use to speak up! Thread your superpowers throughout the language you use to describe yourself. Table 7.2 shows a few example entries from me.

Take the time to complete your own version of this activity. You must understand what makes you great and what superpowers you bring to your leadership. Once you know this, you can work intentionally and deliberately on speaking up and standing out.

Table 7.2: My leadership superpowers

My leadership superpowers	How I use my leadership superpowers
I am a curious observer of people.	I pay attention to the way people are and I am curious about their superpowers, about what makes them great *and* happy. This means I make sure I always have the right person in the right place doing the right thing, both for my team members and for the organisation.
I get shit done!	I am decisive and have a bias for action. I bring this to my leadership by helping my colleagues to realise the importance of forward momentum and celebrating some early wins.

Now, complete this sentence: 'I am known for my [insert the words and phrases that describe your greatness].'

Please write it out repeatedly. From that, your brand will emerge like a butterfly from its cocoon or a beautiful sculpture from a block of stone.

Chapter 8

Speak Up and Stand Out!

Have you ever wondered why you have been overlooked for a promotion? Or why you weren't selected for an interesting cross-functional project? Or why you didn't get to attend the latest training program or conference? You know you do great work, are a great team player and consistently go the extra mile for the organisation. Maybe a boss or mentor has told you that you must raise your profile at work to get ahead, but you weren't entirely sure why they said that.

Perhaps the answer is that no one knows just how talented you are, what your career aspirations are and how much potential you have, because you haven't told anyone!

Research and my work with thousands of women over the past decade tell me that women still struggle with self-promotion. If this feels familiar, then ask yourself these three questions:

1. Do you think your good work, commitment and going the extra mile will get you noticed and promoted?
2. Are you waiting for the perfect time to put yourself forward to discuss your talent, aspirations and potential?

3. Do you feel uncomfortable talking about yourself and your accomplishments?

If you answered 'yes' or 'maybe' to any of these questions, I have some news:

- Your good work (alone) is not enough.
- There is rarely the perfect time to blow your trumpet (although there can be wrong times!).
- Others are self-promoting, and you are being left behind.

Dr Sonja Hood, CEO of Community Hubs and President of the North Melbourne Football Club, put it like this:

> 'The bloke in the desk next to you has his next move planned out, and he's already networking about it. It doesn't matter that he's less skilled than you – the overriding issue for him is his ambition. Ambition is something you should embrace, not avoid.'

As I've already discussed, our male counterparts do not typically feel shy about self-promotion. Men are more likely to take credit for their accomplishments and are comfortable and, dare I say, encouraged to discuss their potential openly. On the other hand, women do not talk up their future potential enough, nor are they encouraged to enough!

Why women must speak up

As I explored in chapter 6, women can be punished more harshly for overt expressions of ambition and aspiration. After all, women have been told for too long to dial it down, wait their turn, stay silent and not play a big game, hearing things like, 'Too big for her boots', 'So bossy!', 'What a show-off!', 'Shameless self-promoter', 'Not very ladylike' and, 'Full of herself'.

Is it any wonder that women are reluctant to get out there and promote their achievements when they experience feedback like this or see other women receiving it? It doesn't surprise me that many women keep their accomplishments to themselves, but it does concern me. These statements are mean, awful tactics to keep women 'in their place' and playing small.

'Tall poppy syndrome' means being cut down when you stand out. This happens when you achieve something big but are met with criticism or judgment instead of celebration of your success. The theory is that your changing stature threatens the status quo.

In 2016, Taylor Swift released the global megahit 'Shake It Off', which she has described as 'a song that I wrote about having to deal with on an everyday basis, just kind of how human beings treat each other'. I wish Taylor Swift had been around when I was in Year 6 at primary school. The class was asked who would like to be school captain the next year when we all graduated to the senior Year 7 class, and I put myself forward. My female schoolmates handed me a lesson swiftly (pardon the pun) about being too big for my boots, being bossy, being a show-off: they ostracised me in class and during recess and lunchtimes for weeks. I was so embarrassed. It was a lesson that remained with me for a long time; I still feel a little anxious when I recall it, even now. My gruesome teenage years, filled with observations of similar behaviour towards other tall poppies, taught me to keep my head down, fit in with the crowd and never speak up or call attention to myself, particularly about my talent and ambition.

Society tells women in many ways that speaking up is not OK. Many of us have been shushed, spoken over or interrupted, or simply cannot get a word in edgewise when some bloke is blathering on and taking up all the oxygen in the room.

We've also seen what happens when prominent women leaders speak up. Many have written about the appalling treatment meted out to Julia Gillard during her term as Prime Minister of Australia, which resulted in her now legendary misogyny speech. Prime Minister Gillard, still the only woman to hold the highest political office in Australia, spoke about the double standards she and other women must endure. I mean, has any male politician ever been publicly criticised for the tone of his voice, the size of his bum or the suit jacket he has worn?

In the lead-up to Australia's referendum on the Indigenous Voice to Parliament, Professor Marcia Langton, a prominent and respected voice for First Nations people in Australia and a supporter of the Yes campaign, was vilified for calling out racism and stupidity in the approach taken by the No campaign. Her words were twisted, and she was told in no uncertain terms to sit down, shut up and remember her place. In the eyes of the pale, stale, male brigade who shouted her down, her place as a Blak woman in Australia sits a long way down the pecking order.

I don't judge you if you aren't uncomfortable standing out and speaking up. You've probably seen and experienced example after example, in the workplace and in society, of women being told they must be compliant and unemotional, and meet behavioural expectations set by a powerful, homogenous group of people that still dominates the halls of parliament, boardrooms and executive tables. No wonder I did not willingly or proactively step up at various times in my career when the limelight beckoned. No wonder other women don't either. The limelight can be harsh, even brutal.

So, we wait for the right time, the right boss and the right role. We wait to be noticed. But the trouble with that tactic is that women often won't be noticed, discovered, anointed or appointed. The people who are noticed, discovered, anointed and appointed are those who have mastered the art of authentic self-promotion. Yep, I'm talking about the bloke in the desk next to you who has his next move planned out and is already networking about it.

As a leader, it is your responsibility to speak up on behalf of the following people and groups:

- **Yourself.** You need to speak up about what you want to those who can give it to you. Managers, sponsors and mentors are not mind-readers (no matter how good you think they are!).

When they ask about your plans or how they can help, you must be ready to tell them. Otherwise, they will stop asking!

- **Your team members.** Leaders are expected to speak up when they see potential risks, problems or opportunities, and represent and advocate for the team's work to more senior people.
- **Those who cannot.** Leaders use their platform of power and privilege to advocate for under-represented, disenfranchised, excluded and marginalised people.
- **Your organisation.** The CFO of an ASX-listed organisation recently told a group of women in my leadership program to 'challenge the status quo more, speak up when you see better ways of doing things'. Another leader I respect says, 'We pay our leaders to have an opinion!'

Speaking up doesn't mean being a self-aggrandising blowhard who takes up all the space in the room, because those people deserve the tall poppy syndrome! Speaking up means always adopting a high-performance-leader mindset by advocating for yourself, others and your organisation.

In the previous chapter, you created your brand statement, which represents your attributes, values and skills. When you speak up, do so in a way that is congruent with your values and how you want to represent yourself.

Are you feeling uneasy about speaking up?

I want to share some honest facts with you if you are feeling uneasy about this.

Self-promotion is a crucial career skill that women should regularly engage in to reach our full potential. Rather than viewing self-promotion as arrogant, we should consider it a necessary aspect of career success. Considering the inevitable boom-bust business cycle (in other words, there will always be good times and tough times) and the shift in the way work is done (face-to-face, remote or hybrid all now being commonplace), having the mindset that self-promotion is crucial is more important than ever before.

You might be thinking, *Well, I am talented, so I'll be OK.* Newsflash: just because someone is talented doesn't mean they will be recognised for their work. As previously mentioned, simply doing good work is not always sufficient. Managers have busy schedules, organisations are spread out, priorities are constantly changing and technology is continuously evolving, all of which can cause talented individuals and groups to be overlooked amid the busyness. Without self-promotion, who is actually going to know about your good work to move the business forward?

I also really want women to understand and embrace the fact that their career success requires a wide network of relationships and an understanding of how to leverage the principles of strategic networking. One such principle is to establish your credibility through the results you deliver and the outcomes you create. Sadly, your boss can't know everything, especially about your accomplishments, and the opportunity for face-to-face or one-on-one meetings to discuss career advancement based on your track record of accomplishments may be limited. Keeping only your boss informed about what you've accomplished only goes so far. Many people across the team and organisation need to know who you are and what you have to offer.

People need to be in roles where they can be most efficient and effective. Long gone are the days when 'just doing your job' translated to success. Everyone is doing more with less, now more than ever. In the tough times, such as when economic downturns at a business, sector or macroeconomic level may lead to downsizing, restructuring and cost-cutting, you make yourself vulnerable if you trust that the leadership group will make the best decisions about your worth to the organisation. The most visible employees often make the cut, but not necessarily the most valuable.

Lean organisations need to employ and keep the best performers. Are you known as one of the best performers? If you haven't committed to self-promotion, then I suggest that you haven't necessarily positioned yourself for ongoing tenure at a minimum.

In other words, all of this is me telling you that you have to sell yourself! But, as Renata Bernarde said on *The Job Hunting Podcast*, 'You don't have to be all grown up and boring!'

Recognition of our inherent strengths is the cornerstone of high-impact, authentic self-promotion, and you've already done most of the heavy lifting to know your strengths, skills, attributes, values and superpowers by now! There is just one additional step: I need you to ensure that you are showcasing your accomplishments. As my wise colleague Susan Colantuono says, 'Don't get accomplishment amnesia!'

What should you speak up about?

Not getting accomplishment amnesia means you have to make time to reflect on what you've accomplished. Here are some thought starters:

- What strengths are you known for?
- What is the best compliment a boss has ever given you?
- What is the best thing a colleague has ever said about you?
- What testimonials have customers provided about you?
- What recognition or honours have you received?
- What are the most important personal goals you have met or exceeded?
- What training or education have you completed that helps you drive your organisation forward?
- What new skills have you developed, and how have they improved your organisation?
- How have you contributed to your profession or industry?
- What are you known as an expert on?
- How have you helped your organisation grow?
- What problems do you solve for your organisation?

When should you speak up?

You should speak up regularly! Remember, doing great work is not enough. You need to communicate effectively about your work, individual contributions and team efforts to achieve your long-term career objectives. I want to emphasise that we are discussing all types of goals, not only your personal ambitions. Speaking up in service of yourself, others and your organisation is key to great leadership. Here are some ideas about when you can discuss your personal, professional, team and organisational accomplishments:

- When you get a new boss
- At skip-level meetings
- At town hall meetings
- At your annual performance evaluation
- In one-on-one meetings with your boss
- At team meetings
- During progress updates with clients or stakeholders
- At industry meetings, workshops or conferences
- Online (via LinkedIn or in-house social media)
- On your CV
- When you are asked!

Discussing your accomplishments with poise and without embarrassment will stand you in great stead as your career progresses. If you have an opportunity to take your organisation forward through your thought leadership, you need to share that! Research from *Catalyst* found, 'When women were most proactive in making their achievements visible they advanced further, were more satisfied with their careers, and had greater compensation growth than women who were less focused on calling attention to their successes'.

How should you speak up?

The language used when self-promoting and showcasing accomplishments makes all the difference. Right now, I want to direct you to the book *No Ceiling, No Walls* by Susan Colantuono, and specifically the chapter 'The Language of Power™'. In brief, the language of power is the language of business; so, when discussing accomplishments, it's helpful to use powered-up language about how you've moved the business forward. Table 8.1 shows some examples.

Table 8.1: Powered-up language

Instead of this...	Try this...
'I've pulled together a great cross-functional team. It's the first time we've done it.'	'I'm pleased that I was able to assemble a talented cross-functional team that delivered the project ahead of time so we could start collecting revenue earlier than planned.'
'I have a great team. They do fabulous work.'	'This quarter, my team managed to boost sales by 25% and improve customer retention to 97%.'
'I put in a lot of effort this year.'	'I am proud to report that I have consistently achieved or exceeded every milestone in support of our strategic profitability goals.'
'I'm an accountant,' or, 'I'm a risk manager.'	'I help executives make winning business decisions,' or, 'I help our leaders make decisions that keep our company safe.'
'I managed 150 people and a $27 million budget.'	'I increased revenue by 35% per year while maintaining our existing cost profile.'
'Oh, it was nothing,' or, 'My team deserves all the credit.'	'Thanks.'

SOURCE: ADAPTED FROM *NO CEILING, NO WALLS*

As Maya Angelou said, 'When I talk about the things I've achieved, I'm not bragging on me, I'm bragging on the rainbows in my clouds.'

The art of storytelling can't be underestimated when considering how to (better) sell yourself and your accomplishments. I quite like the Dragon-Slaying Story method by Liz Ryan. This method comprises the following three steps:

1. What went wrong
2. What you did to solve the problem
3. The happy result – the proof that the action you took was the right one.

For example:

'I am proud of the time when [problem or opportunity you encountered] I was able to [the solution to the problem or opportunity], which meant that [the outcome you delivered or impact you had].'

Here is a true story:

'I am proud of the time that I gathered my entire team, plus all our outsourced partners, for the first time together to map our end-to-end supply chain so we could identify the process gaps impeding the strategic project. My leadership in that moment ensured that the large, complex team could create new ways of working so that we delivered our $100 million project on time and within budget.'

The back story is that I was the executive in charge of a major technical program for one of Australia's major banks. I had been parachuted into the role to remediate a failing project that had significant implications for our customers, shareholders and reputation if it was not delivered on time. Against much resistance from internal stakeholders, I asked for the entire project team, including suppliers who were competitors, to come together to hear what was needed from them and why, and ask them to co-create a solution for what had the potential to become a high-profile failure. It worked – we delivered on time and without spending a single cent more than was required.

Get into the habit of telling your success stories with trusted people over dinner, coffee breaks or team meetings. Starting will feel awkward, but remember, you're learning a new skill, so give yourself a break! Your authentic voice will flow naturally with time, and before you know it you'll be confidently showcasing how you've contributed to your colleagues and the organisation.

There is no substitute for practice. So, once you are more confident, graduate to telling these stories at work, in meetings, at coffee catchups and, importantly, when talking with your boss. Remember the ripple effect. Encourage other women to learn this technique, and make space for them to speak up and stand out!

Go deeper

I've detailed here ten steps that can help you speak up and stand out, which are also aligned with the Advancing Women Formula:

1. **Show commitment to CPD and the company by investing time in learning new skills.** Ask your boss for development recommendations to improve your skills, or express interest in taking on special projects to stretch yourself and help the company achieve its strategic and financial goals.

2. **Focus on the team's success, not just your own.** Senior leaders value collaboration among team members, so foster an inclusive and psychologically safe environment, because that will create a high-performance team that is aligned to the organisation's goals.

3. **Know your numbers!** Understand your positional purpose (why the firm invests in your role) and be ready to discuss how to move key performance metrics forward. Prove the value of

your contributions, own your failures and adopt a 'no excuses' mentality. This self-awareness is a mark of great leadership.

4. **Do what you say, and do it well.** Executives look for people with a good track record of delivering positive results. Establish a reputation for high-quality work by hitting home runs on small projects. This could lead to bigger opportunities later.

5. **Think strategically.** The best leaders balance working 'on' the business with working 'in' the business. When working 'on' the business, look beyond to-do lists and focus on opportunities that help achieve the strategic and financial goals of your organisation. This means considering the big picture when making decisions.

6. **Challenge the status quo and suggest new solutions.** If you have a fresh idea or a creative solution to meet a new challenge, share it openly. People who identify problems and suggest at least one solution that is aligned with the organisation's goals are the ones who get noticed and given more responsibility.

7. **Consistently improve your communication skills, particularly when it comes to executive communication.** Be thoughtful, adapt to the audience, follow up to understand expectations and, of course, enhance your executive presence.

8. **Build relationships throughout the company.** Expand your network, gain allies and increase your influence. Great leaders put themselves in positions where they're more likely to be consulted. Work collaboratively and cross-functionally, and your name will come up for all the right reasons.

9. **Become known as an ethical and trustworthy colleague.** Lead through your values and those of the organisation, and inspire others to follow. Demonstrate your commitment to values-based leadership by discussing values when making decisions and in meetings, appreciating colleagues and highlighting how projects align with the organisation's values and purpose.

10. **Ask!** Put your hand up for opportunities to showcase your skills. Display initiative and volunteer to contribute to areas that align with the organisation's strategic initiatives. Clearly explain how you can add value and what you stand to gain. Your boss wants to place you where you can make the greatest impact.

For each step, work through the following action points:

- Assess whether each step is a strength or a gap for you.
- Write a brief example of the behaviours relating to this step that you consistently demonstrate in your role.
- Identify the behaviours relating to this step that you need to start, stop or continue to achieve success in your current role.
- Discuss this with your boss or strategic mentor and ask their advice on what else to consider undertaking (especially if you are approaching an appraisal, performance review or, if you are ready for your next role, career discussion).
- Build the agreed actions into your career plan.

Chapter 9

How to Network Like a CEO

Networking is synonymous with speaking up and essential for a soaring career. The more senior you become in your career, the greater the expectation that you will be an accomplished networker with extensive networks. When you're a CEO, you're the number-one salesperson for your organisation, so you must be skilled at building and leveraging strategic networks to move the organisation forward.

We must also be our number-one salesperson as individuals (remember: sell yourself!) and be skilled at building and leveraging strategic networks to move our careers forward. This chapter covers the mindset and skills for in-person networking and the power of social media for networking, specifically LinkedIn.

Networking mindsets

People often ask me how I became skilled at networking. I respond that I changed my negative mindset and practised regularly.

I used to dread attending events alone and initiating conversations with strangers, fearing being left wandering aimlessly like a lonely child at a new school. So, I avoided networking events like the plague and didn't initiate any networking activities myself. I used to be snobbish about attending business networking events required for my career advancement and seniority. I didn't enjoy them and, frankly, thought they were a necessary evil. Back in those days, my mindset was that networking was showing up to an event, making awkward small talk, exchanging business cards and fending off pushy people trying to sell me something.

Do you think that networking is a necessary evil? Do you mutter to yourself 'I hate networking' when you're invited to participate in a networking event or activity?

If you answered 'yes', know you are not alone. It can be tough to shift your approach to networking, but it's an important step towards progress. An attitude and mindset adjustment can unlock your potential and the opportunity to advance your brilliant, soaring career.

Networking is working

I learned that networking is working when I left Telstra and took a role in the private sector in 2005. After initially turning up my nose in distaste at the obligatory networking events I attended, I had a couple of light-bulb moments that altered my mindset about networking:

1. I was responsible for growing the business, and I became acutely aware that people do more business with people they know, like and trust – and not enough people in the industry and potential client organisations knew me! So, how could I grow the business if I shied away from building mutually beneficial relationships?
2. I needed to get inside my head, work out what was going on and get serious about what was necessary for my job and managing my brand. I needed a mindset change.

I decided to examine my mindset first. If you must do this, I highly recommend reading *Mindset* by Stanford University Professor Carol Dweck. This book was a great reminder to me to choose my attitude daily. Another choose-your-mindset tool that I appreciate is the FISH! Philosophy. The main takeaway is that your mindset is something you can choose. Even simple things like attending a networking event with a curious mindset can lead to significant changes. You may learn something new about someone you've never met, which can be a real game changer.

Networking skills

I was on my way to shifting my mindset about networking, so now I needed some skills and techniques to help me overcome the awkwardness when I met someone new. A useful technique that I came across was to have a set of questions in my mental back pocket to ask new people I meet. It's a great way to get to know people, and most people don't mind chatting about themselves! But first, I practised with my family!

I used this technique during dinnertime when my kids were in school. Instead of asking the usual questions like 'How was your day?' or 'What happened today?', which would only get a short answer, I would ask them open questions such as 'What's one thing you learned today that you didn't know yesterday?' This approach worked a treat and helped us have more meaningful conversations. We soon started to see a bit of healthy competition between brother and sister about who could provide the day's most colourful, interesting update. (I travelled a lot, too, so this was a great strategy for the nightly telephone call.) I could see that this approach of asking an open question that makes people interested to respond was working, so I started using it in my everyday networking when meeting new people.

You should develop your own set, but here are a few of my trusted go-to questions that go beyond talking about the weather and the football!

- What's the best career advice you've ever been given?
- When you were 15, what were your career aspirations?

- What do you love most about your role?
- How did you earn your first pay packet?
- If you could spend an hour with anyone in the world, who would it be?

As a leader, having a 'networking is working' mindset matters. Your approach and reactions to networking will leave an impression on those around you. Imagine this scenario: You return to your workplace from a networking event and your team members ask how it went. Rather than expressing a negative sentiment like 'I hated it and wished I didn't have to go', it would be more positive to say something like 'I met someone fascinating who might be able to help us to...'

However, it's important to remember that attending events is just one small aspect of networking.

My journey with LinkedIn

I was recognised as one of the AFR 100 Women of Influence 2018 for advocating for gender diversity, equity and inclusion (DEI). I felt a deep sense of pride and accomplishment and knew that this award would do wonders for my professional brand and credibility.

As a woman of influence, I frequently contemplate the impact I can make. I am resolutely committed to empowering women and girls around the globe, and I leverage every available avenue, including LinkedIn and other social media platforms, to amplify my mission and achieve my goals.

In 2016, when I decided to dive into full-time self-employment, I broadcasted my new venture on LinkedIn. To my astonishment, the post gathered over 65,000 views and garnered more than 500 comments. Almost eight years later, the post continues to engage people.

This experience underscored two crucial things: first, the immense potential of LinkedIn, and second, the undeniable fact that when women shape their brand with purpose, they create lasting impacts in both personal and professional spheres. LinkedIn has been a strategic channel for me to stand out and speak up for nearly 15 years, and I am eager to share my LinkedIn story with every woman out there.

I won't claim to be a LinkedIn expert, as I've mainly learned through trial and error. However, having been recognised as a LinkedIn Top Voice twice and having a substantial following (over 18,000 people at the time of writing), I'm likely to be doing something right.

Where are all the women?

It's hard not to notice that LinkedIn reverberates with male voices. Women account for between 43 and 44% of LinkedIn users, so the potential for women to stand out by speaking up on LinkedIn is high.

Here are some interesting statistics about LinkedIn that women should consider:

- There are 950 million users on LinkedIn, including 194 million in the USA, 34 million in the UK, 20 million in Canada and 13 million in Australia.
- Eight people are hired through LinkedIn every minute.
- LinkedIn is used by 77% of recruiters regularly to source candidates.

LinkedIn has become one of the most powerful tools for professionals to network, gain industry insights and create a soaring career. While everyone can benefit from LinkedIn, professional women stand to gain in several ways. Let's explore why.

LinkedIn offers everyone, regardless of gender, a fair chance to connect with professionals in their industry. This inclusivity fosters a supportive atmosphere where women can find mentors, sponsors and opportunities to advance their careers. Plus, LinkedIn provides a wealth of resources, such as articles, courses, webinars and other tools, to help people develop vital leadership skills such as networking and learn from leaders worldwide. It's always encouraging to see a platform that's committed to helping people reach their full potential.

It's important for women to have a strong professional image and be recognised as thought leaders in their fields. LinkedIn provides an excellent platform for women to showcase their insights, publications and accomplishments to a wide audience. Additionally, several professional groups on LinkedIn cater specifically to women, offering a safe space to access resources, advice and networking opportunities. Joining these groups can be highly valuable for mutual growth and support. The other advantage of a global platform like LinkedIn is that you can connect with professionals from diverse locations, which can broaden your horizons, providing access to more opportunities and perspectives.

To enhance your visibility in your industry, it's important to actively engage in discussions, post regularly and interact with other people's content. Companies often use LinkedIn to find potential candidates, and by keeping your profile up to date and being active on the platform you can increase your chances of being discovered and contacted by recruiters who might otherwise over-rely on traditional, homogeneous networks. The long-term effect of more women making themselves visible to recruiters in this way is that it creates more opportunities to close the recruitment gender gap.

Every woman should have the opportunity to become a respected authority in their chosen field and have control over their career path. LinkedIn is more than just another social media platform; when used strategically, it has the potential to help you to stand out and speak up. As marketing strategist Bonnie Power says, 'LinkedIn is a pivotal platform for executive women to establish their brand and network with key decision-makers. Begin by actively seeking opportunities so you're always in a position to dictate your career's trajectory'.

You might be doing fine with occasional LinkedIn logins and sporadic posts, but if any of the following statements resonate with you, take them as a wake-up call to rejuvenate your LinkedIn strategy:

· I haven't refreshed my LinkedIn profile in the last six months.
· My headline doesn't encapsulate my unique value.

- My LinkedIn URL isn't customised.
- I don't have a current professional headshot on my profile.
- I haven't engaged with posts by strategic connections in the past month.
- I haven't shared any insightful content recently to underscore my expertise.
- I haven't been proactive in expanding my strategic network.
- I haven't recommended any strategic contacts lately.

Women have told me that they lack the time, confidence and skills to use LinkedIn more fully. Prioritising 'me' time is an onerous task for many women, but given that LinkedIn is such a powerful channel, I hope to inspire you to act.

How to take action

You might be reading this and thinking, *But I am OK. I access LinkedIn from time to time. I post occasionally.* Nope! It is not enough. You must dedicate time every month to standing out and speaking up. Laura Ryan, the global Chair of Meat Business Women, a huge network for women and their organisations in the meat industry, says to 'spend two hours of dedicated work time monthly on your network and personal brand'.

Molly Beck, author of *Reach Out: The simple strategy you need to expand your network and increase your influence*, spends 15 minutes once a week writing emails or LinkedIn messages to people to extend and nurture her network. She has four different types of Reach Out:

1. **The Re-Reach Out:** reconnecting with a lapsed connection without guilt or shame.
2. **The Follow-up Reach Out:** the first contact after the first contact.
3. **The Borrowed Connection Reach Out:** leapfrogging across your network to friends of friends.
4. **The Cool Reach Out:** the vulnerably courageous ask to connect with someone you admire but who doesn't (yet) know you.

Molly writes, 'There is deep power in digging into your network to push yourself toward your professional dreams, and most of that power is through acquaintances whom you know loosely, individuals whom you've met in passing, and friends of friends'.

The bottom line is that whatever method you choose, you must make time! Block out time in your calendar that you can devote to this necessary career-building task.

LinkedIn housekeeping

When I invite people to my home, I make sure they have the correct address, I provide directions and I make sure that my home is ready to receive guests – clean and tidy being the basics. It's the same with your online networking. Make sure your LinkedIn profile is ready to receive guests by being easy to identify as yours, having up-to-date information and accurately representing your professional brand.

If you're looking to boost your LinkedIn profile, here's a helpful guide for auditing it. These steps can help you attract more visitors, and stand out and speak up!

First of all, tidy up your profile:

- If you have not reviewed your LinkedIn profile in the last six months to ensure it is up to date and represents your CEO brand. Do this first.
- Ensure the headline (the line below your name) is updated to reflect your brand statement, not just your role title.
- Customise your LinkedIn URL. You can check out LinkedIn's Quick Tips to find out how.
- Please ensure you have an up-to-date, professional headshot on your LinkedIn profile. No selfies or shots with sunglasses or a glass of champagne!
- If you're not confident updating your LinkedIn profile, enlist help! There are many experts out there. I recommend one of our fabulous members in the Lead to Soar network, Renata Bernarde.

Now, allocate time in your calendar each week to standing out and speaking up on LinkedIn (30 minutes for the first couple of weeks, and then you can drop it back to 15 minutes):

- Review your notifications and manage any connection requests you have. If you are tagged in posts by other people, they will show up here. Go to the posts and either hit a reaction or make a comment.
- Respond to any direct messages you have received.
- Search for posts by strategic connections and react or comment.
- Post an interesting article, with a summary or commentary to demonstrate your expertise and thought leadership.
- Search for and invite people to your LinkedIn network. Choose thought leaders and experts in sectors you're interested in and people who you think can help you or who you can help.

Becoming proficient in a skill requires dedication and repetition, and gaining the confidence to be an active two-way user of LinkedIn is no different. I want more women to become highly sought-after authorities in their preferred fields and be free to choose their career path.

There is another thing to consider about using LinkedIn (and networking): although you may feel comfortable in your current job, nobody can guarantee that the status quo will remain so. What happens if there is restructuring or your role is made redundant? These two things happen regularly in the corporate world. How are you positioned to manage the risk or leverage the opportunity?

Having a large, diverse network of people will position you for greater choice when things happen at work that are outside your control, as well as when you want to make career moves. This is yet another reason why I recommend incorporating LinkedIn into your daily routine. There is no superior (and free) public forum than LinkedIn for cultivating your CEO brand and building a soaring career.

Go deeper

OK, by now you're aware that I am a massive fan of reflective practice. Take the time now to consider the quality and diversity of your professional networks online (such as LinkedIn) and in real-life settings. How might they (better) fuel your soaring career?

1. Reflect on where you are in your career right now. How has your network of connections helped you with your progression? What have you learned from those people and about yourself?

2. For each connection, briefly note how they have contributed to your professional growth and advancement. This could be through mentorship, industry insights, collaboration opportunities, targeted introductions or sponsorship. Write this down.

3. What would you like to accomplish in your career over the next 12 months? Write this down.

4. Now, consider how your current connections can help you achieve these goals. Write this down.

5. Now, create a SMART action plan to tap your existing network. SMART action plans are specific, measurable, achievable, relevant and time-bound. Then, JFDI (just frickin' do it)!

Want to go even deeper? Download my 'Network Like a CEO' audit and action plan so that you can build, enhance and leverage your strategic network to add rocket fuel to your career.

michelleredfern.com/thank-you-for-purchasing-my-book

Chapter 10

Fixing the System (not Women)

What does it mean to fix the system, exactly? Is the system people, behaviour, processes or technology?

It is all the above.

When considering strategies for closing the global leadership gender gap, I often think about this quote:

> 'When a flower doesn't bloom, you fix the environment, not the flower.'

I think about flowers not blooming when asked to run events such as leadership-development or confidence-building workshops for women. If you've skipped to this part of the book, you won't have read me calling bullshit on the idea that women aren't confident, aren't ambitious and don't want leadership roles – they do, and the evidence for that is strong. Please go back and read chapter 6 now if you haven't yet.

When I began leading the Game Changers women's leadership program at IAG in 2018, I alerted the Australian executives and program coordinators to the possibility of unintended consequences, such as middle-management women leaving IAG after participating in the program. I was advised to do this by my wise friend Susan Colantuono, who has witnessed numerous organisations focus solely on 'fixing women' programs without addressing systemic issues. Susan has seen countless women discover their potential and capability through her programs only to be held back by gender bias and discrimination in the workplace. As a result, when many of these confident women uncovered just how talented, competent and credible they were, they voted with their feet and chose to find employment elsewhere, where their worth was recognised and their careers could advance.

Are you considering how to close the leadership gender gap in your organisation and develop the capability and capacity of the women in your talent pipeline? This chapter focuses on how organisations can address gender bias and discrimination in the workplace environment and provide career-advancing development opportunities for women.

Examining the environment (not the flower)

Two organisations that I worked for in my corporate career had safety as their number-one value. One of those organisations sent workers out in vans and trucks, up poles, down pits, under houses and onto roofs. The other organisation had workers in mines, oil rigs, ships and manufacturing environments. Both organisations wanted all workers to be safe and go home at night alive and as healthy as they left their families and homes that morning. They were deliberate, mindful and process-driven about keeping their people safe.

The leaders of those organisations, me included, were accountable for living and breathing safety as our number-one value by role-modelling deliberate, mindful, purposeful and process-driven safety behaviours. This resulted in both excellent safety metrics and, most importantly, more team members returning to their homes safely after each shift.

Imagine if the inclusion and advancement of women was considered as important as safety back then; what might my experience, and that of the women around me, have been? At that time in my career, the early 2000s, women were still largely relegated to junior, supportive, administrative roles. While I was a senior manager then, I was the only woman on the senior leadership team (and not for the first time in my career). I constantly battled blatant and subtle sexism, from being spoken over in meetings, to being asked to take notes in meetings, to being told that because I hadn't come up through the technical ranks I had no business having an opinion on how to run that part of the business.

When it comes to creating and sustaining an environment that works for women, the same mindset and behaviours as prioritising safety apply. Living and breathing gender equity as a number-one value means role-modelling deliberate, mindful, purposeful and process-driven gender equity behaviours.

Now, you can substitute whatever metric you like here – revenue, profit, customer satisfaction or anything else. What would happen in your organisation if women were as important as that metric? Again, take the time to reflect on what you will do about that. Because until workplace gender equity is made a priority, women will still be subjected to unacceptable mindsets, behaviour and processes.

The book *Good Guys: How men can be better allies for women in the workplace* posits that men are the missing ingredient in gender equality, and that more men need to move beyond just being a 'good guy' and start doing more. The authors, David G Smith and W Brad Johnson, rightly call out that it's great to be a bloke because men built the workplace for men to do men's work.

This 'built for men' factor covers everything from the temperature of rooms through to the equipment being designed for 'one size fits men', as pointed out by Caroline Criado Perez in her book *Invisible Women: Data bias in a world designed for men*, including personal protective equipment (PPE), which women are still being asked to wear despite it often being detrimental to their safety and the safety of those around them. During the COVID-19 pandemic, there were countless stories of women in medical environments having to wear ill-fitting PPE that could have resulted in the transmission of the very disease they were trying to treat. Similarly, women tell me they are expected to wear safety goggles and gloves that are far too large because the smallest size is a man's small, which engulfs them and does not effectively keep them safe.

While these examples relate to the physical environment of workplaces, there are non-physical 'one size fits men' factors prevailing in workplaces. This chapter explores those factors and how managers can fix the environment so women can have careers that soar in their workplace, not someone else's!

How to fix the system (not the women)

Management is dominated by men (see figure 10.1), so this chapter is aimed fairly and squarely at the more than the 70% of people in leadership who are men. Men in management are largely the missing ingredient in gender equity, and given fish rots from the head, it is men's choice whether their organisations will rot or flourish. Dr Sonja Hood, CEO of Community Hubs and President of the North Melbourne Football Club, told me, 'Game-changing leadership sees how things could be and uses where things currently are as a starting point, not as a limitation'.

Game-changing leaders are deliberate, mindful and process-driven about women in their workplace because they know that by doing so, they will reap the benefits of a high-performance workplace. There are more statistics, research, case studies and evidence than I have had hot dinners to prove that having more women at the top is better for women and their families, businesses, the economy and society.

The Bankwest Curtin Economics Centre (BCEC) has partnered with the Australian Workplace Gender Equality Agency (WGEA) to help close the gender gaps in workplaces in Australia. In 2020, BCEC published research demonstrating that more women in leadership had a positive causal effect on business performance. The research demonstrated that profitability, performance and productivity increase under female leadership, and female top-tier managers add 6.6% to the market value of ASX-listed companies, and so it concluded that female leadership will help businesses thrive in a post-COVID-19 world.

Figure 10.1: The global leadership gender gap

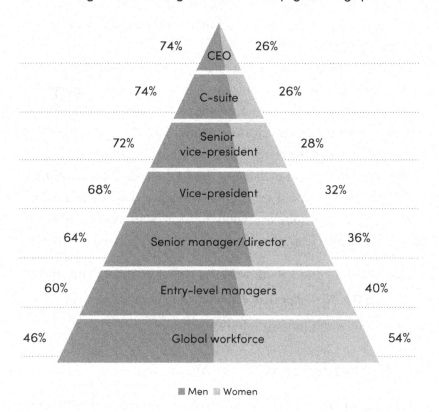

	74%	CEO	26%	
74%		C-suite		26%
72%		Senior vice-president		28%
68%		Vice-president		32%
64%		Senior manager/director		36%
60%		Entry-level managers		40%
46%		Global workforce		54%

■ Men ■ Women

Why does this outperformance occur as a result of more women in leadership? Because it means more:

· diverse perspectives, backgrounds and approaches in the workplace, which can lead to better decision-making

- collaborative and democratic management techniques, which can improve decision-making and promote corporate social responsibility

- involvement of stakeholders and promotion of information sharing, which can lead to a stronger commitment to corporate social responsibility and better performance during times of crisis.

As Chair and Managing Director of the International Monetary Fund (IMF) Christine Lagarde wrote, 'As I have said many times, if it had been Lehman Sisters rather than Lehman Brothers, the world might well look a lot different today'.

Game-changing leaders know that intersectional gender balance in organisations is no longer a nice-to-have. It is no longer acceptable not to have DEI and the advancement of women embedded in the strategy and operating cadence of organisations. It is no longer best practice not to value the contributions of women in the workplace.

In other words, game-changing leaders are deliberate, mindful and process-driven about creating a workplace that works for (all) women. These questions are good thought starters, and a game-changing executive team should consider them regularly:

- How do women feel about working at your company, and why?
- What is the lived experience of women in your workplace?
- Does your workplace work for women?

Not another fixing women program!

Imagine if Serena Williams hadn't been mentored or hadn't done training drills. Would she have won 23 Grand Slam women's singles titles and become arguably the best female tennis player ever?

Imagine if Australian Rules football star Daisy Pearce hadn't turned up for training. Would she have been the AFL Women's (AFLW) inaugural number-one draft pick in 2013, the inaugural captain of Melbourne Football Club's AFLW team, a Best and Fairest (equivalent to MVP) winner and, after her retirement, a respected coach and commentator?

Both women will have had a strategy for their careers and executed it in a disciplined way to secure their lauded positions. Their strategies will have included securing the right coaching, training, mentoring and sponsorship appropriate at each stage of their careers.

In my experience as both a veteran of corporate workplaces and now someone who guides and advises organisational leaders about how to close the leadership gender gap, few organisations approach developing the women in their talent pipeline in a similarly disciplined way. There is a systematic lack of *strategic* training, coaching, mentoring and sponsorship in organisations for women.

I emphasise 'strategic' because continually updated research from Susan Colantuono shows that when notable research about leadership considers women's strengths, just 9% of the attributes and skills associated with women relate to BQ skills. Conversely, when we consider the leadership strengths of men, there is an overrepresentation of BQ skills and much less representation of EQ and SQ skills (see figure 10.2).

Figure 10.2: Perceptions of men's and women's leadership skills

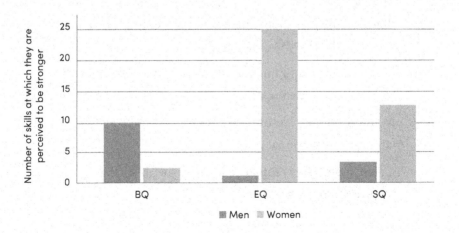

Why is this important? Because at least 50% of the criteria associated with executive and C-suite roles relate to BQ. I asked LinkedIn to assist me in writing a CEO job description; here is the generic template provided:

Sample CEO job description

[Company X] is looking for an experienced and dedicated chief executive officer who can lead the team with an effective business strategy that optimises the company's growth. The ideal candidate will assume responsibility for the staff, oversee team initiatives and help make robust, data-driven corporate decisions that elevate the company's financial and operational performance. As the senior leader at [Company X], the chief executive officer will foster a positive, inspiring and collaborative work environment that empowers employees to actively work towards company-wide goals.

Objectives of this role:

- Be the key representative of the company in communicating important decisions to business stakeholders and the public

- Manage the company's overall development and ensure that general operations run seamlessly as employees accomplish established goals

- Make strategic and financial decisions that determine the trajectory of the company

- Monitor budgets, resources and procedures by working with cross-functional teams

- Create a positive company culture through strong, inspirational leadership.

Responsibilities:

- Develop, execute and assess top business strategies that will propel company growth

- Collaborate with other executives, managers and employees to identify meaningful solutions

- Serve as the main resource for managers in finance, marketing and sales operations

- Adjust important procedures and policies by collaborating with HR and assessing current industry trends.

Required skills and qualifications:

- Expert understanding of corporate finance and business management

- Strong knowledge of financial, technical and economic concepts

- Proven success as a senior executive managing departmental teams

- Familiarity with regional regulatory compliance

- Excellent communication skills.

Preferred skills and qualifications:

- Relevant certification in business administration or equivalent experience in corporate management

- Collaboration skills for establishing positive working relationships

- Ability to work under pressure to meet deadlines and accomplish business objectives

- Project management skills.

Then, I categorised each of the skills in the job description as BQ, EQ or SQ. Unsurprisingly (to me, anyway), 83% of the skills required by a CEO are BQ skills (see table 10.1).

Table 10.1: CEO skills categorised as BQ, EQ and SQ

Objectives of this role	
Be the key representative of the company in communicating important decisions to business stakeholders and the public	BQ/SQ
Manage the company's overall development and ensure that general operations run seamlessly as employees accomplish established goals	BQ
Make strategic and financial decisions that determine the trajectory of the company	BQ
Monitor budgets, resources and procedures by working with cross-functional teams	BQ/EQ
Create a positive company culture through strong, inspirational leadership	EQ/SQ
Responsibilities	
Develop, execute and assess top business strategies that will propel company growth	BQ
Collaborate with other executives, managers and employees to identify meaningful solutions	EQ/BQ
Serve as a main resource for managers in finance, marketing and sales operations	BQ
Adjust important procedures and policies by collaborating with HR and assessing current industry trends	EQ/BQ

Required skills and qualifications	
Expert understanding of corporate finance and business management	BQ
Strong knowledge of financial, technical and economic concepts	BQ
Proven success as a senior executive managing departmental teams	BQ/EQ
Familiarity with regional regulatory compliance	BQ
Excellent communication skills	EQ/SQ
Preferred skills and qualifications	
Relevant certification in business administration or equivalent experience in corporate management	BQ
Collaboration skills for establishing positive working relationships	EQ
Ability to work under pressure to meet deadlines and accomplish business objectives	EQ/BQ
Project management skills	BQ

Total CEO skills	**18**
Total BQ skills	**15**
% of CEO skills that are BQ skills	**83%**

In addition, as I continue to discover when facilitating women's leadership development programs, the career advice being directed to women fails to address the need for women to develop and demonstrate BQ. I maintain a database of responses to the question, 'What is the best career advice you have ever been given?' Women tell me the career advice they receive is typically from a manager, mentor or coach. Shockingly, even in 2023, the advice that women receive and pay attention to overemphasises EQ and SQ and largely ignores BQ (see figure 10.3). Just 4% of the advice that women tell me they receive relates to building and demonstrating the critical business skills that constitute more than 50% of the criteria for executive roles and, as we saw earlier, 83% of the skills associated with C-suite roles.

Figure 10.3: Career advice given to women

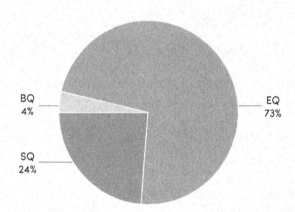

BQ
4%

EQ
73%

SQ
24%

Therefore, it is time for organisational leaders to examine the efficacy of the coaching, training and mentoring they provide to women in their talent pipeline.

Managers must give the right advice

Why are women systematically not being coached, trained, mentored and sponsored in our organisations? One reason is that not enough managers are coached, trained and mentored to develop 21st-century DEI leadership skills, which means that they are likely not to give women well-rounded career advice. When I say well-rounded, I mean that at least 50% of the coaching, training and mentoring they offer to women must be related to developing and demonstrating BQ.

As I have just mentioned, the majority of the coaching, training and mentoring that women receive falls into the categories of EQ and SQ:

- **EQ** includes engaging team members, building collaboration and developing successful relationships with clients and stakeholders. Indeed, managers rank women as outperforming their male peers in this area of leadership.
- **SQ** includes building confidence, raising your profile and displaying executive presence.

Women also receive a large proportion of their career advice – formal and informal – from their line manager, because most learning and development happens 'on the job'.

However, there is another type of advice that women receive far more than their male counterparts. Women (and marginalised people) receive feedback more often about their 'personality', not their performance. Research by Textio with 25,000 respondents across 253 organisations shows that this type of personality politics holds women back and contributes to the leadership gender gap. This spells bad news for organisations should they not pay attention, because people subjected to such low-quality feedback are 63% more likely to contemplate leaving their current place of employment. Clearly, this is an issue when organisations are trying to plug the holes in a leaky talent pipeline of women, and it reinforces the need to provide training to managers at every career stage about how to coach, train, mentor and develop women more effectively, which includes offering 'specific, relevant and actionable' feedback 'with clear examples and clear suggestions for improvement'.

A great way to start combating this problem is by asking yourself, *Would I give this advice to a senior male employee?*

Not another mentoring program!

When I speak at an event, post blogs or articles, or attend networking events, women invariably tell me they do not have a mentor and ask how they can get one, or that they've been told to 'get a mentor' as part of their career advice. When I ask them why they want a mentor or have been told to get one, most assume that mentoring is the key to unlocking their potential.

Sometimes, when an organisation reaches out to me for a potential engagement, it is to help them design and facilitate a mentoring program for women. I always ask why the organisation has chosen to run a mentoring program for women. Most assume that a mentoring program is the key to closing the leadership gender gap.

My response to both groups of people is always the same: 'Women are over-mentored and under-promoted.'

In 2022, I posted a graphic on LinkedIn stating that women are over-mentored and under-promoted, and it is fair to say it went viral. The last time I checked the post, it had received 214,000 views, 2876 reactions and 161 comments and was reposted 58 times. I have reposted the same graphic and sentiment several times and it hits a nerve each time, with many people wanting to tell me what I already know: that a mentoring relationship can be a developmental partnership through which one person shares knowledge, skills, information and perspectives to foster someone else's personal and professional growth. I agree that this type of relationship is valuable, but it cannot close the leadership gender gap alone. Gaining a mentor or participating in a mentoring program is unlikely to result in a woman being promoted because, as Herminia Ibarra put it in a 2019 *Harvard Business Review* article, 'While a mentor is someone who has knowledge and will share it with you, a sponsor is a person who has power and will use it for you'. Women are not benefiting from sponsoring programs as much as men, who are being promoted at a faster pace.

I interviewed Cindy Gallop, a high-profile advocate for gender-equal, diverse and inclusive workplaces, on the *Lead to Soar* podcast in 2022, and she told listeners that women don't need mentors; they need champions, people who are going to make things happen for their career. She and Tomas Chamorro-Premuzic expanded in a *Harvard Business Review* article about their (and my own) distrust of mentoring (alone) by saying that we should strike the word 'mentor' from our vocabulary because mentoring alone will not create forward movement in a woman's career. That is the job of a career 'champion' or sponsor:

> 'Women need what men get all the time – someone prepared to go out on a limb for them. A champion is someone who, behind closed doors, slams their fist on the boardroom table and says, "If there's only room for one bonus in the budget, it's going to Jane, not John".'

Carla Harris, an executive at Wall Street firm Morgan Stanley, teaches us about sponsors in her TED Talk 'How to Find the Person Who Can Help You Get Ahead at Work'. She says to forget meritocracy; it doesn't exist. (I fervently agree, and you can contact me to find out why!) The notion that working hard, having your head down and your bottom up, will get you promoted is complete BS. Sure, you must deliver the goods – that is, meet and exceed your performance measures – but the truth is that you also need someone in the room who will speak for you.

What is 'the room'? The room is where your boss, their boss and their peers make talent-related decisions. Who gets the pay rise? Who gets the lion's share of the bonus pool? Who gets the promotion, secondment or plum assignment? Who is chosen for succession planning? Who is chosen for high-potential talent development programs? The list goes on.

It is unlikely that a woman will be in the room when decisions about her career are being made. So, she must have a sponsor to speak for her in that room, someone who will 'spend their currency' of social and political capital on her and pound the table on her behalf.

Is a mentor going to pound the table for her? This is highly unlikely because, as Harris points out, a conventional mentor (warm, fuzzy, supportive) is unlikely to be in the room. However, the woman may have a sponsor in the room pounding the table on her behalf if the following five factors have been addressed:

1. The woman has built a track record of accomplishment *and* invested in building strategic relationships with people who can help her career advance. (Um, hello? Networking?)

2. The woman has planned her mentoring relationship strategically, and her mentor has been carefully selected to be both a person in the room and skilled enough to help her enhance her BQ competencies.

3. The mentor has ensured that the woman has developed and demonstrated her BQ skills. The demonstration of her skills must be particularly evident to those in the room.

4. The mentor has been trained in the art of strategic mentoring of women and has interrupted the gendered mindsets and gender biases they hold.

5. The mentor has agreed to put their social and political capital on the line for the woman by proactively advocating for her at every opportunity.

Now, I ask you: does your organisation's women's development program or mentoring program for women address these five criteria? If so, great – you've provided the women in your talent pool the best possible chance to secure a sponsor. If not, then I'll restate it for those in the back:

'Women are over-mentored and under-promoted!'

This means that instead of yet another women's mentoring program, the organisation must invest in designing a high-impact, measurable sponsorship program for women. A sponsorship program is not easy to develop and implement successfully, but it is not impossible. It must feature a highly curated 'hothouse' of talented women, powerful executives and skilled facilitators to ensure that women have the best possible chance of advancing and the organisation has the best possible chance of closing its leadership gender gap.

Diversity, equity and inclusion skills

Leaders must acquire 21st-century DEI skills. It's essential to understand that DEI is not solely the responsibility of the DEI lead, consultants or the human resources department. Leaders should take ownership of DEI and consider it a leadership competency, like any other, that can be honed through discipline and practice.

First, let's look at some terminology about the fundamentals of DEI:

- **Diversity** can be defined as the range of human differences, including but not limited to gender, race, sexual orientation, disability and age. Diversity is the first step to DEI for most organisations as it addresses who employees are but not how their work experiences differ.
- **Equity** is the concept that all employees deserve the same opportunities to grow, develop and achieve while acknowledging that certain groups face advantages and others face barriers, which creates imbalances. As people come from different starting points, equity recognises that organisations must adjust practices to meet people where they are.
- **Inclusion** ensures that employees of all identities feel welcomed, valued and actively engaged. An inclusive workplace ensures that each individual feels like they're a part of the collective and that each member is given the same rights and opportunities.
- **Belonging** occurs when employees feel secure, supported and empowered to be their authentic selves at work. A key outcome

of inclusion, belonging directly impacts how engaged and committed someone feels at work.

- **Intersectionality** refers to how different aspects of a person's identity interact and intersect in unique ways. These different identities – such as gender, race, sexuality, disability and age – can reduce or compound the (dis)advantages somebody faces at work and in society. Building a diverse, equitable and inclusive workplace requires policies and practices acknowledging employees' whole selves.

- **Gender bias** is the tendency to give preferential treatment to one gender over another. It can be conscious or unconscious, and it can manifest in a variety of ways. Gender stereotyping comes from gender bias and assumes that all members of a particular gender have certain characteristics or abilities – for example, assuming that all women are nurturing or all men are good at maths.

- **Microaggressions** are brief, everyday exchanges that communicate hostile, derogatory or negative messages to a person based on their marginalised group membership. They are often unintentional, but they can have a lasting impact on the person who experiences them.

- **Unconscious bias** means holding implicit beliefs about people's capabilities or roles that are not based on reality – for example, believing that women are not as ambitious as men or that men are better suited for leadership roles.

To be successful as a leader, it's crucial to have a solid grasp of all significant business metrics and the ability to analyse and interpret them effectively. Failing to acquire and refine these skills can hinder your performance and hurt your organisation's overall success. DEI metrics are business metrics, and the more diverse, equitable and inclusive your organisation is, the more likely it will deliver positive business outcomes.

Effective leaders prioritise six DEI areas that poor management often overlooks.

1. DEI strategy and implementation plan

Poor management often neglects the development of a meaningful DEI strategy or implementation plan. They make statements such as these:

'There's no budget for DEI.'

'We've got other priorities.'

'We don't have a problem because [insert excuse here].'

'The employee resource group will take care of that.'

Effective leaders understand the importance of a workplace where DEI is embedded into business strategy and operations, actively seek to create an inclusive culture and encourage diverse perspectives to thrive.

2. Recruitment and hiring processes

Poor management accepts that bias is baked into recruitment and hiring. It perpetuates this by continuing to accept statements such as 'we only hire on merit' or 'this is the best person for the job' from hiring managers.

Effective leaders ensure that the organisation's recruitment strategy, policies and processes are continuously reviewed through a DEI lens and that hiring managers are provided with training on hiring inclusively.

3. Performance evaluations

Poor management can perpetuate bias through performance evaluations that lack transparency and objectivity. Poor management allows performance management systems, processes and practices to occur without standardisation and scrutiny of the subjectivity of the rater. A lack of a DEI lens on evaluations can result in women and people from other marginalised communities being over-looked for promotions and pay rises despite their qualifications and accomplishments.

Effective leaders develop transparent, objective and standardised performance evaluation processes to mitigate bias and ensure equitable treatment for all employees, regardless of identity.

4. Formal talent and career management pathways

Poor management fails to develop equitable formal talent and career management pathways. When equitable access to development and advancement opportunities is lacking, bias will thrive. Women and other marginalised folks, particularly those in male-dominated workplaces, will face challenges such as exclusion from high-profile projects and strategic mentorship or sponsorship.

Effective leaders proactively address inequity in talent management systems and processes. They hold other leaders accountable for the growth and advancement of women and other marginalised folks to address imbalance with robust review processes when developmental opportunities arise.

5. Support for working families

Poor management allows rigid gender stereotypes to dictate policies about the intersection between team members' work and home lives. Poor management also fails to recognise that society burdens women disproportionately with unpaid labour, which can affect their career progression. Poor management overlooks the importance of creating a family-friendly work environment that accommodates the needs of all employees, regardless of gender.

Effective leaders know that families come in all shapes and sizes. They also acknowledge that team members (of all genders) have different needs and measure the performance of team members by the outcomes they generate, not by their attendance in the office.

Effective leaders regularly audit and update workplace policies and practices to be family-friendly.

6. DEI accountability and metrics

Poor management fails to establish accountability mechanisms and metrics to track progress towards workplace gender equity. Without clear aspirations and metrics, there is no DEI 'north star', which results in no action, fragmented actions or ineffective activity misaligned with the business strategy.

Effective leaders hold themselves accountable for creating an inclusive workplace, set measurable goals and regularly assess progress against the goals to ensure continuous improvement.

It's time to call it

While gender bias has deep roots in societal structures, poor management practices play a significant role in perpetuating and sustaining gender (and other) disparities in the workplace. By calling this what it is, management underperformance, we can ensure that organisations become effective at adopting inclusive practices and taking substantive steps toward creating equitable environments that enable women and other marginalised folks to reach their full potential.

Final points on fixing the environment (not women)

There are three key points that summarise how to fix the environment and not women:

1. Effective management is important to ensure everyone at work is engaged, especially women. When managers focus on taking care of all members of their team and ensuring everyone feels included, women are more likely to feel satisfied with their jobs and less likely to feel burnt out. They're also more likely to

recommend their company as a great workplace and less likely to think about leaving, which helps the organisation attract and keep talented women employees.

2. Managers with well-developed BQ, EQ and SQ competencies are more likely to ensure that women (and other marginalised people) are coached, trained, mentored and sponsored in a way that results in them achieving their full potential.

3. Organisations that adopt a strategic, disciplined approach to developing leaders with BQ, EQ and SQ skills are more likely to close their leadership gender gap and ensure they sustainably outperform relative to their peers.

When it comes to the advancement of women, I want more organisational leaders to take a leaf from the playbooks of Serena Williams and Daisy Pearce and ensure their organisation has a winning strategy. That means they must, at minimum, do the following things:

- **Commit.** CEOs and executives must commit to creating and sustaining workplace gender equity. Be visible and vocal about the organisation's commitment to gender equity.

- **Know the current state.** CEOs must know as much about women's representation and lived experience in their workplace as they do about the financials. Confront the brutal facts.

- **Collect data.** Even a basic spreadsheet can help organise information. Don't wait to start – incomplete data is better than no data.

- **Assess both qualitative and quantitative data.** Considering the perspectives of women colleagues in your workplace as well as quantitative data (such as statistics around the representation of women across management layers or employee engagement survey data split by gender) is highly recommended to gather meaningful insights. This rounded approach can offer a valuable data pool and will assist in creating targeted interventions.

- **Diagnose!** Don't spend a cent until you're clear on the problem you're trying to solve and the opportunities that must be leveraged. Where are the issues for women? What is working well for women? What must the organisation do more or less of for women?
- **Set targets.** A successful business is all about targets and measures. CEOs must create a vision and a target state for workplace gender equity. They must measure the impact and progress of their workplace gender equity strategy against the target state.
- **Assign accountability.** Gain buy-in from the executive team for a workplace that works for women. Hold the entire leadership team accountable for being active and vocal advocates for gender equity and delivering the strategy.
- **Stay curious and keep listening.** CEOs must remain respectfully curious and not assume they know all the problems and all the solutions. They must be disciplined about regularly listening to learn. CEOs who do this are the most successful in moving workplace gender equity from conversation to action.

Go deeper

Game-changing leaders continue to challenge the status quo and ask questions to ensure the organisation maintains its competitive edge. This section includes some resources you may wish to ask your leaders to use to better support women in your workplace.

Executive team discussion and reflection

Open the conversation with your executive leadership team by stating your vision for a more diverse, equitable and inclusive workplace. Ask the team to adopt a growth mindset and help uncover where there are risks and opportunities when it comes to women in the workplace using the following prompts – what might the organisation look like, sound like and feel like if:

- gender equity was a high priority?
- executive and senior leader scorecards measured gender equity performance?
- regular workplace gender equity audits were conducted?
- the workplace recognised, rewarded and celebrated behaviours that promote gender equity?
- gender equity was the first agenda item for all organisational meetings?
- there was gender balance at all levels of leadership?

Use inclusive leadership practices to ask and gain responses to each of these questions. Pay attention to the quietly powerful people in the room who speak up the least but are worth listening to when they do! Ensure that people with different communication styles and preferences can contribute in a way that works for them. You can download a 'Leaders Guide to Inclusive Meetings and Inclusive Brainstorming' resource from the companion website. Gather the responses, develop actionable insights and collectively decide on the leadership commitments.

To go even deeper, download the 5X5 Discussion Guide to help you start the journey towards diversity, equity and inclusion:

michelleredfern.com/thank-you-for-purchasing-my-book

About the Author

Michelle Redfern, the driving force behind Advancing Women in Business and Sport and Lead to Soar, is deeply committed to closing the global leadership gender gap. Her extensive knowledge about the multifaceted benefits of gender parity – socially, organisationally and economically – enables her to expertly craft and implement comprehensive gender equality strategies for both corporate entities and sports organisations.

An expert in diversity, equity and inclusion (DEI), Michelle has been recognised with numerous awards for her impact. She frequently lends her voice and insights as a host and speaker at various events, including leadership forums, conferences and diversity-focused gatherings.

In addition to her consulting and speaking roles, Michelle designs and facilitates strategic mentoring programs and women's leadership development initiatives. Her efforts are underpinned by a strong belief in the transformative power of equipping women with the tools and opportunities necessary to excel in leadership positions.

As the author of *The Leadership Compass: The ultimate guide for women leaders to reach their full potential*, Michelle encapsulates her extensive experience and commitment to fostering a world where women's leadership is acknowledged, actively nurtured and celebrated.

References

Preface: I Am a Leader

Clancy, L & Austin, S, 'Fewer Than a Third of UN Member States Have Ever Had a Woman Leader', Pew Research Center, 28 March 2023,pewresearch.org/short-reads/2023/03/28/women-leaders-around-the-world.

Introduction: Business, Emotional and Social Intelligence

Colantuono, S, 'The Career Advice You Probably Didn't Get', video, TEDxBeaconStreet, November 2013, ted.com/talks/susan_colantuono_the_career_advice_you_probably_didn_t_get.

id., *No Ceiling, No Walls: What women haven't been told about leadership from career-start to the corporate boardroom*, Interlude Productions, 2010.

id., *Make the Most of Mentoring: Capitalize on mentoring and take your career to the next level*, Interlude Productions, 2012.

Salovey, P & Mayer, JD, 'Emotional Intelligence' *Imagination, Cognition and Personality*, vol. 9, no. 3, March 1990, pp. 185–211.

Goleman, D, *Emotional Intelligence: Why it can matter more than IQ*, Bantam Books, New York, 1995.

id., *Working with Emotional Intelligence*, Bantam Doubleday Dell, New York, 2008.

id., *Social Intelligence: The new science of human relationships*, Random House, New York, 2006.

Chapter 1: Who Are You Called to Become?

Fox, C, *Stop Fixing Women: Why building fairer workplaces is everyone's business*, NewSouth Publishing, Sydney, 2017.

Catalyst, 'Women in Management (Quick Take)', 1 March 2022, catalyst.org/research/women-in-management.

Lara, S, Baird, M & Hood, R, *Progress and Barriers in Global Gender Leadership*, LinkedIn Economic Graph, April 2023, economicgraph.linkedin.com/content/dam/me/economicgraph/en-us/PDF/global-gender-representation.pdf.

Workplace Gender Equality Agency, 'The ABS Data Gender Pay Gap', accessed 28 November 2023, wgea.gov.au/data-statistics/ABS-gender-pay-gap-data.

id., *Australia's Gender Equality Scorecard: Key results from the Workplace Gender Equality Agency's Employer Census 2021–22*, December 2022, wgea.gov.au/sites/default/files/documents/WGEA-Gender-Equality-Scorecard-2022.pdf.

World Economic Forum, 'Global Gender Gap Report 2023', 20 June 2023, weforum.org/reports/global-gender-gap-report-2023/in-full/gender-gaps-in-the-workforce.

Chapter 2: Leadership that Gets Results

Althoff, S, 'Men Named Jo(h)n Have Written as Many of 2020's Top Business Books as All Women combined', *Fortune*, 21 December 2020, fortune.com/2020/12/20/women-bestselling-business-books-2020.

Enron: The smartest guys in the room, motion picture, Magnolia Home Entertainment, Los Angeles, 2005.

Kunti, S, 'Crashing Down: A decade of corruption cripples FIFA', *Forbes*, 28 December 2019, forbes.com/sites/samindrakunti/ 2019/12/28/crashing-down-a-decade-of-corruption-cripples-fifa.

Topham, G, 'The Volkswagen Emissions Scandal Explained', *The Guardian*, 24 September 2015, theguardian.com/business/ ng-interactive/2015/sep/23/volkswagen-emissions-scandal-explained-diesel-cars.

Chang, D & Hartill, R, 'The Subprime Mortgage Crisis of 2008: A beginner's guide', *The Ascent*, updated 26 October 2023, fool.com/ the-ascent/mortgages/subprime-mortgage-crisis.

Reserve Bank of Australia, 'The Global Financial Crisis', accessed 28 November 2023, rba.gov.au/education/resources/explainers/ the-global-financial-crisis.html.

Watkins, MD, 'Demystifying Strategy: The what, who, how, and why', *Harvard Business Review*, 10 September 2007, hbr.org/2007/09/ demystifying-strategy-the-what.

Hatami, H & Hilton Segel, L, 'What Matters Most? Six priorities for CEOs in turbulent times', McKinsey & Company, 17 November 2022, mckinsey.com/capabilities/strategy-and-corporate-finance/our-insights/what-matters-most-six-priorities-for-ceos-in-turbulent-times.

Telstra, *Telstra Annual Report 2023*, 1 September 2023, telstra.com.au/aboutus/investors/reports.

Mankins, M & Steele, R, 'Turning Great Strategy into Great Performance', *Harvard Business Review*, July–August 2005, hbr.org/2005/07/turning-great-strategy-into-great-performance.

@VAndthriving, social media post, 5.59 p.m., X, 27 January 2021, twitter.com/VAndthriving/status/1354323036573323267.

Chapter 3: Metrics that Matter

LinkedIn Learning, 'Finance and Accounting Online Training Courses', accessed 28 November 2023, linkedin.com/learning/topics/finance-and-accounting.

Chapter 4: Lead Yourself

Tjan, AK, 'How Leaders Become Self-Aware', *Harvard Business Review*, 19 July 2012, hbr.org/2012/07/how-leaders-become-self-aware.

Dweck, C, 'What Having a "Growth Mindset" Actually Means', *Harvard Business Review*, 13 January 2016, hbr.org/2016/01/what-having-a-growth-mindset-actually-means.

'Self-compassion: Dr. Kristin Neff', accessed 28 November 2023, self-compassion.org.

Goleman, D & Boyatzis, RE, 'Emotional Intelligence Has 12 Elements. Which Do You Need to Work On?', *Harvard Business Review*, 6 February 2017, hbr.org/2017/02/emotional-intelligence-has-12-elements-which-do-you-need-to-work-on.

English Oxford Living Dictionaries, 'Vulnerability', accessed 18 January 2018, en.oxforddictionaries.com/definition/vulnerability.

Brown, B, *Daring Greatly: How the courage to be vulnerable transforms the way we live, love, parent, and lead*, Gotham Books, New York, 2012.

Gallup, 'Employee Engagement', accessed 28 November 2023, gallup.com/394373/indicator-employee-engagement.aspx

Redfern, M, '9 Things I've Learned About Following My Bliss', LinkedIn, 30 April 2023, linkedin.com/pulse/9-things-ive-learned-following-my-bliss-michelle-redfern.

Chapter 5: Lead Others and Organisations

Kotter, JP, 'What Leaders Really Do', *Harvard Business Review*, December 2001, hbr.org/2001/12/what-leaders-really-do.

Bennett, N & Lemoine, GJ, 'What VUCA Really Means for You', *Harvard Business Review*, January–February 2014, hbr.org/2014/01/what-vuca-really-means-for-you.

Zenger, J & Folkman, J, 'Research: Women score higher than men in most leadership skills', *Harvard Business Review*, 25 June 2019, hbr.org/2019/06/research-women-score-higher-than-men-in-most-leadership-skills.

Porter, J, 'Why You Should Make Time for Self-Reflection (Even If You Hate Doing It)', *Harvard Business Review*, 21 March 2017, hbr.org/2017/03/why-you-should-make-time-for-self-reflection-even-if-you-hate-doing-it.

Goleman, D, 'What Makes a Leader?', *Harvard Business Review*, January 2004, hbr.org/2004/01/what-makes-a-leader.

Clarke, A, *Future Fit: How to stay relevant and competitive in the future of work*, 2nd edition, Major Street Publishing, Melbourne, 2021.

Goleman, D, 'Leadership That Gets Results', *Harvard Business Review*, March–April 2000, hbr.org/2000/03/leadership-that-gets-results.

Chapter 6: Confidence Conundrum

@kashia, social media post, Instagram, 27 April 2021, instagram.com/p/COK1B4iHLXF.

O'Connell Rodriguez, S, 'Forget the ambition gap, it's the "ambition penalty" that's *really* holding women back at work', *Glamour*, 16 January 2023, glamourmagazine.co.uk/article/ambition-penalty.

Chamorro-Premuzic, T, *Why Do So Many Incompetent Men Become Leaders? (And how to fix it)*, Harvard Business Review Press, 2019.

id., 'Why Do So Many Incompetent Men Become Leaders?', *Harvard Business Review*, 22 August 2013, hbr.org/2013/08/why-do-so-many-incompetent-men.

Dunning, D & Kruger, J, 'Unskilled and unaware of it: how difficulties in recognizing one's own incompetence lead to inflated self-assessments', *Journal of Personality and Social Psychology*, vol. 77, no. 6, January 2000, pp. 1121–1134.

Reuben, E, Rey-Biel, P, Sapienza, P & Zingales, L, 'The emergence of male leadership in competitive environments', *Journal of Economic Behavior & Organization*, vol. 83, no. 1, June 2012, pp. 111–117.

Chaplin TM, 'Gender and Emotion Expression: A Developmental Contextual Perspective', *Emotion Review*, vol. 7, no. 1, January 2015 pp. 14–21.

Svendsen, H, *Take on Board*, podcast, helgasvendsen.com.au/take-on-board-podcast.

Chapter 7: Be Your Own CEO

Morse, G, 'The Science Behind Six Degrees', *Harvard Business Review*, February 2003, hbr.org/2003/02/the-science-behind-six-degrees.

Chritton, S, 'Personal Branding For Dummies Cheat Sheet', *Dummies*, updated 26 February 2022, dummies.com/article/business-careers-money/careers/general-careers/personal-branding-for-dummies-cheat-sheet-207677.

Parsons, T, 'The #1 Thing Your Personal Brand Needs To Convey', *Work It DAILY*, 13 September 2016, workitdaily.com/personal-brand-needs-convey.

kevan.org, 'Johari Window', accessed 21 December 2023, kevan.org/johari.

Gallup CliftonStrengths®, 'Live Your Best Life Using Your Strengths', accessed 28 November 2023, gallup.com/cliftonstrengths/en/home.aspx.

Redfern, M, 'Hello My Name is …. How to Nail a Confident Self-Introduction', podcast episode, *Lead to Soar*, 10 October 2022, shows.acast.com/lead-to-soar/episodes/63fed0074be61300121fa5ee.

Chapter 8: Speak Up and Stand Out!

Exley, CL & Kessler, JB, 'The Gender Gap in Self-Promotion', working paper, National Bureau of Economic Research, revised May 2021, nber.org/papers/w26345.

Waheed, J, '11 Best Taylor Swift Songs That Prove She's the Ultimate Country-pop Icon', *Glamour*, 19 July 2023, glamourmagazine.co.uk/article/taylor-swift-best-songs.

ABC News (Australia), 'Julia Gillard's "misogyny speech" in full (2012) | ABC News', video, YouTube, 8 October 2012, youtube.com/watch?v=ihd7ofrwQX0.

Radio National Breakfast, radio program, Australian Broadcasting Corporation, 13 September 2023, abc.net.au/listen/programs/radionational-breakfast/marcia-langton-says-no-campaign-are-using-fear-over-fact-/102848462.

Bernarde, R, 'The 5 Things No One Tells You About Job-hunting', podcast episode, *The Job Hunting Podcast*, 16 May 2022, thejobhuntingpodcast.com/post/don-t-be-boring.

Catalyst, 'The Myth of the Ideal Worker: Does Doing All the Right Things Really Get Women Ahead?', 1 October 2011, catalyst.org/research/the-myth-of-the-ideal-worker-does-doing-all-the-right-things-really-get-women-ahead.

Ryan, L, 'How Dragon-Slaying Stories Will Help You Get The Job', *Forbes*, 7 March 2017, forbes.com/sites/lizryan/2017/03/07/how-dragon-slaying-stories-will-help-you-get-the-job.

Chapter 9: How to Network Like a CEO

Dweck, C, *Mindset: The new psychology of success*, Ballantine Books, New York, 2008.

FISH! Philosophy, 'What is Fish?', accessed 28 November 2023, fishphilosophy.com/what-is-fish.

Australian Financial Review Women of Influence, 'Michelle Redfern', accessed 28 November 2023, live.afr.com/womenofinfluence/alumni_search/michelle-redfern.

Dixon, SJ, 'Distribution of LinkedIn users worldwide as of January 2023, by gender', *Statista*, 22 February 2023, statista.com/statistics/933964/distribution-of-users-on-linkedin-worldwide-gender.

LinkedIn Pressroom, 'About Us: Statistics', accessed 28 November 2023, news.linkedin.com/about-us#Statistics.

Beck, M, *Reach Out: The simple strategy you need to expand your network and increase your influence*, McGraw Hill, New York, 2017.

Chapter 10: Fixing the System (not Women)

Smith, DG & Johnson, WB, *Good Guys: How men can be better allies for women in the workplace*, Harvard Business Review Press, 2020.

Criado Perez, C, *Invisible Women: Data bias in a world designed for men*, Harry N. Abrams, New York, 2019.

Porterfield, C, 'A Lot Of PPE Doesn't Fit Women—And In The Coronavirus Pandemic, It Puts Them In Danger', *Forbes*, 29 April 2020, forbes.com/sites/carlieporterfield/2020/04/29/a-lot-of-ppe-doesnt-fit-women-and-in-the-coronavirus-pandemic-it-puts-them-in-danger.

Criado Perez, C, 'Another Truth from the Covid Inquiry: Women were being ignored over ill-fitting PPE long before the pandemic', *The Guardian*, 4 November 2023, theguardian.com/commentisfree/2023/nov/03/covid-inquiry-women-ill-fitting-ppe-pandemic-unisex-healthcare.

On the Tools, 'One Size Does Not Fit All: The problem with PPE for women', accessed 28 November 2023, onthetools.tv/the-problem-with-ppe-for-women.

References

Cassells, R & Duncan, A, 'Gender Equity Insights 2020: Delivering the business outcomes', presentation at the BCEC|WGEA Equity Insights 2020 Report Launch Event, 19 June 2020, bcec.edu.au/assets/2020/06/BCEC-WGEA-2020-Presentation-June-2020-FINAL.pdf.

Lagarde, C, 'Ten Years After Lehman—Lessons Learned and Challenges Ahead', *International Monetary Fund*, 5 September 2018, imf.org/en/Blogs/Articles/2018/09/05/blog-ten-years-after-lehman-lessons-learned-and-challenges-ahead.

Nedera, S, 'What is Intersectionality? And Why is It Important for Gender Equality?' *UNDP Bosnia and Herzegovina*, 27 May 2023, undp.org/bosnia-herzegovina/blog/what-intersectionality-and-why-it-important-gender-equality.

Twomey, C, 'Pearce the First Pick in AFL's Inaugural Women's Draft', *Australian Football League*, 16 May 2013, afl.com.au/news/2013-05-16/daisy-plucked-first.

Colantuono, S, 'The Missing 33%: Has anything changed?', LinkedIn, 7 February 2023, linkedin.com/pulse/missing-33-has-anything-changed-susan-colantuono.

Zenger, J & Folkman, J, 'Research: Women score higher than men in most leadership skills', *Harvard Business Review*, 25 June 2019, hbr.org/2019/06/research-women-score-higher-than-men-in-most-leadership-skills.

Textio, 'New Data Reveals that Low-quality Feedback Makes Your Team Want to Quit', accessed 28 November 2023, textio.com/feedback-bias-2023.

Ibarra, H, 'A Lack of Sponsorship Is Keeping Women from Advancing into Leadership', *Harvard Business Review*, 19 August 2019, hbr.org/2019/08/a-lack-of-sponsorship-is-keeping-women-from-advancing-into-leadership.

Ibarra, H, Carter, NM & Silva, C, 'Why Men Still Get More Promotions Than Women', *Harvard Business Review*, September 2010, hbr.org/2010/09/why-men-still-get-more-promotions-than-women.

'Blowing Shit Up with Cindy Gallop', podcast episode, *Lead to Soar*, 14 November 2022, shows.acast.com/lead-to-soar/episodes/blowing-shit-up-with-cindy-gallop.

Gallop, C & Chamorro-Premuzic, T, '7 Pieces of Bad Career Advice Women Should Ignore', *Harvard Business Review*, 15 April 2021, hbr.org/2021/04/7-pieces-of-bad-career-advice-women-should-ignore.

Harris, C, 'How to Find the Person Who Can Help You Get Ahead at Work', *TEDWomen 2018*, November 2018, ted.com/talks/carla_harris_how_to_find_the_person_who_can_help_you_get_ahead_at_work.

Index

strengths 42–45, 53, 62, 63, 69, 90, 93, 101–103, 106–107, 115, 139
stress 76
sub-prime scandal 27
success xi, 5, 7, 13–14, 20, 24, 29, 37, 40, 42, 52, 56, 72, 75, 92, 113, 114, 119, 150, 155
—barriers to xi, 8, 14, 20, 33, 85, 149
Svendsen, Helga 33, 38, 94
Swift, Taylor 111
SWOT analysis 42–45

talent management 14, 20, 23, 32, 91, 134, 139, 144, 145, 147, 148, 152
tall poppy syndrome 111, 113
teamwork 64
TED Talks xi, 6, 147
Telstra 11–12, 18, 35, 47–49, 76, 89
threats 33, 40, 42–45
Trump, Donald 86

trust 12, 13, 74–76, 80, 120
Twitter 100

UCMS 48–49, 51, 53, 55, 89, 98
United Nations 2
United States Armed Forces 81

values 36, 69, 83, 101, 106, 120
vision 32, 34, 35, 36, 38, 72, 75, 78–79, 82, 155
Volkswagen 27
Voltaire 81
VUCA (volatility, uncertainty, complexity and ambiguity) 73, 80
vulnerability 64–68, 83, 87

Watkins, Michael D 34
weaknesses 42–45, 54, 69
Williams, Serena 138–139, 154
Women of Influence 104, 126
working families 152–153
Workplace Gender Equality Agency (WGEA) 136

Working with Michelle

Michelle knows her clients want high-impact activity that has the ability to engage stakeholders from all levels of the organisation. When your organisation works with Michelle it will:

- be able to demonstrate the strategic and business benefits of an inclusive culture
- create psychologically safe environments for team members to learn more about workplace DEI
- create aha moments about the business risks of ignoring DEI
- enable cross-functional teams and departments to collaborate and work in alignment on solving DEI challenges
- identify ways to attract more people from target markets to the organisation
- enable women in the talent pipeline to develop and demonstrate critical business and leadership skills
- enable people leaders to develop and demonstrate 21st-century inclusive leadership skills.

@   contact@michelleredfern.com
f   facebook.com/AdvancingWomeninBizandSport
○   instagram.com/michelleredferndotcom
X   twitter.com/RedfernMichelle
in   au.linkedin.com/in/michelleredfern

Be better with business books

MAJOR STREET

We hope you enjoy reading this book. We'd love you to post a review on social media or your favourite bookseller site. Please include the hashtag #majorstreetpublishing.

Major Street Publishing specialises in business, leadership, personal finance and motivational non-fiction books. If you'd like to receive regular updates about new Major Street books, email info@majorstreet.com.au and ask to be added to our mailing list.

Visit majorstreet.com.au to find out more about our books (print, audio and ebooks) and authors, read reviews and find links to our Your Next Read podcast.

We'd love you to follow us on social media.

in linkedin.com/company/major-street-publishing

f facebook.com/MajorStreetPublishing

⊙ instagram.com/majorstreetpublishing

✕ @MajorStreetPub